What Could Possibly Go Wrong?

My Life's Journey

Autobiography of the
Author of the Heptalogy:
The Loveday Method

By
Geoffrey Loveday

MAPLE
PUBLISHERS

What Could Possibly Go Wrong? My Life's Journey

Author: Geoffrey Loveday

Copyright © 2025 Geoffrey Loveday

The right of Geoffrey Loveday to be identified as author of this work has been asserted by the author in accordance with section 77 and 78 of the Copyright, Designs and Patents Act 1988.

First Published in 2025

ISBN 978-1-83538-607-1 (Paperback)
978-1-83538-608-8 (Hardback)
978-1-83538-609-5 (E-Book)

Book cover designed and layout by: Geoffrey Loveday

Published by:
Maple Publishers
Fairbourne Drive, Atterbury,
Milton Keynes,
MK10 9RG, UK
www.maplepublishers.com

A CIP catalogue record for this title is available from the British Library. All rights reserved. No part of this book may be reproduced or translated by any form or by any means, electronic or mechanical, including photocopying, recording or by any information storage and retrieval system without written permission from the author.

The novel is entirely a work of fiction. The names, characters, and incidents portrayed in it are the work of the author's imagination. Any resemblance to actual persons, living or dead, events or localities is entirely incidental. The views expressed by the fictional characters do not necessarily reflect the views of the author.

Contents

About the Author 9

Inspiration 11

Dedication 14

Chapter 1: The Beginning 16

Chapter 2: The Real Me 18

Chapter 3: This Is My Story, And It's Time to Share It 20

Chapter 4: Where It All Started 23

Chapter 5: My First Grand Entrance 27

Chapter 6: My Grandfather, and what I learned following him into the cellar 30

Chapter 7: The day I ran away from my dad: Never again, too much pressure 32

Chapter 8: The Not-So-Great Ear Adventure: Five Years of Syringes, Needles, and a Bruised Bum 37

Chapter 9: The Day I Tried to Fly… through a Glass Door 45

Chapter 10: The Day I Picked a Fight with a Brick Wall (and Lost) 48

Chapter 11: Learning My Lesson: You Think? No Way 52

Chapter 12: The Day I Outsmarted Mrs. Birch… Kind Of. 53

Chapter 13: Happy Times: My Unforgettable Childhood 55

Chapter 14: From Parliament Street to Paradise: Moving to Gateacre Park Drive 57

Chapter 15: A New Adventure at King David High: Football Dreams, Hebrew Drills, and the First Crush 59

Chapter 16: The day I fell in love, I was only ten 61

Chapter 17: The Night I Traded Milk for Whiskey, and Paid the Price (With a Broken Nose) 66

Chapter 18: The Quiet Strength of a Mother's Love: A Journey through Faith, Fear, and Unspoken Battles 69

Chapter 19: The day my world was turned upside down..... 76

Chapter 20: A sadness that cut deep 82

Chapter 21: Jackie, who changed my life; and she had no idea how much.. 89

Chapter 22: This was the moment when everything changed 102

Chapter 23: Sadness that stays with you for a lifetime..... 112

Chapter 24: The Great Bunk Bed Incident: How I Almost Turned a School Trip into a Crime Scene 114

Chapter 25: The Amazing (and Often Ridiculous) Journey of My Life.. 118

Chapter 26: The Munchkin Men Strike Again: Shanna's Birthday Surprise Gone Wrong!.................................... 120

Chapter 27: Dinner Disaster: The Day I Became the Main Course.. 122

Chapter 28: The Yellow Mini Bomb Scare: Who Needs Enemies with Advice Like This? 125

Chapter 29: The chandelier explodes into a million tiny pieces, raining down 127

Chapter 30: Sale of the century 132

Chapter 31: The Door Deal of a Lifetime 134

Chapter 32: The Day I Turned a Luton Van into a Convertible: A Masterclass in Chaos................................ 161

Chapter 33: Hanging On for Dear Life—and Laughing About It.. 164

Chapter 34: The Day My Flintstones Minivan Met Its Match: What Could Possibly Go Wrong?......................... 166

Chapter 35: The Time I Nearly Died Over a Free Meal (How to Be the Dumbest Person in the Restaurant) 169

Chapter 36: How I'm Still Standing (Somehow) 173

Chapter 37: The Honeymoon Shenanigans: What Could Possibly Go Wrong?... 175

Chapter 38: The Casino and the Toilet: What could possibly go wrong?.. 178

Chapter 39: The Day My Brother Let Me Near a Brand New Van (It Didn't End Well) 181

Chapter 40: Jackie Always Said 'What Could Possibly Go Wrong?'... And Boy, Did I Prove Her Wrong! 187

Chapter 41: The Great Mouse Hunt: A Night to Remember 190

Chapter 42: The Great Poo-tastrophe: Josh and Zak's Two-Minute Masterpiece 194

Chapter 43: Here we go again: The Time I Hijacked a Stranger's Car 198

Chapter 44: The Hill Start from Hell: How I Nearly Got Flattened by a Runaway Car 200

Chapter 45: My Life as the Universe's Punchline 203

Chapter 46: Speke Market Catastrophe 205

Chapter 47: The Great Gear Disaster: How I Nearly Destroyed a Car, My Wallet, and My Relationship 213

Chapter 48: My Auntie and Uncle Nearly Had a Heart Attack 218

Chapter 49: Should I Still Ask for My Wages? 224

Chapter 50: What Could Possibly Go Wrong? - The Chronicles of My Ridiculous Survival 229

Chapter 51: The Cost of Keeping Me Away: A Financially Sound Decision 231

Chapter 52: How I Nearly Turned a Welding Job into an Action Movie 244

Chapter 53: £29,500 for a Luxury Rat Hotel 247

Chapter 54: The Window Sale That Turned Into a Muddy Meltdown: It's Not My Fault! 253

Chapter 55: A Journey Through Shadows: The Story I've Been Afraid to Share 257

Chapter 56: A Promise through the Years: Carrying Her Love Forward 266

Chapter 57: The Day Life Tested Me Beyond Measure 268

Chapter 58: A Heart-breaking Choice; The Sacrifice Only a Parent Could Make 271

Chapter 59: Embracing the Chaos; A Life Full of Laughter and Surprises 273

Chapter 60: What could possibly go wrong, right? 275

Chapter 61: A Journey through Life's Challenges 280

Chapter 62: The Three-Piece Suite Disaster: My Joyride from Hell 285

Chapter 63: The Great Car Heist Fiasco: What Else Could Possibly Go Wrong? 296

Chapter 64: Why Do These Things Always Happen to Me? 300

Chapter 65: How Tight Jeans Nearly Ruined My Life 302

Chapter 66: Hooked on Trouble: How I Keep Falling for Zak's 'Brilliant' Ideas 304

Chapter 67: Trust Me, It Wasn't Just Zak—Then Came Josh, and Together They Became the Double Trouble Duo! 309

Chapter 68: The Ruby Ring: A Precious Memory Passed Down 311

Chapter 69: The Secret Commando Wound: How a 10-Year-Old Cowboy Healed Himself 314

Chapter 70: My holiday from hell 318

Chapter 71: The Day Everything Changed: A Heart Attack at 70 328

Chapter 72: Why I'm Writing This 330

Chapter 73: A lasting love letter 331

Chapter 74: Let the Magic Begin: Embracing Every Moment Together 335

Chapter 75: A 12-Year-Old's Wild Crossbow Adventure ... 336

Chapter 76: Facing the Unbearable: My Journey through Pain and Silence 338

Chapter 77: Bonfire Night Gone Wrong; The Sparkler Mishap That Thankfully Left No Mark! 345

Chapter 78: Bournemouth Bound and Broke; How I Got Talked into a Rodeo by My Scheming Wife 347

Chapter 79: How I Nearly Drowned Trying to be Superman 356

Chapter 80: Nightmare on Cliffside: How Jackie's Adventures Followed Me to My Dreams! 359

Chapter 81: How My Romantic Horseback Ride Turned into a High-Speed Nightmare 361

Chapter 82: The day I knocked myself unconscious: Everyone was laughing except Jackie – she never spoke to me for two weeks 365

Chapter 83: Never again; But somehow I don't think so .. 371

Chapter 84: Standing Strong; Navigating Debt and Loss as a Single Parent of Five 378

Chapter 85: The Hypnosis Horror Show; When the Unknown Speaks 382

Chapter 86: The Day I Nearly Flew Off a 4-Story Roof; A True Dockside Disaster 394

Chapter 87: From Fresh to Frantic: The Day I Accidentally Bathed in Vim 397

Chapter 88: The gas leak with the darts 399

Chapter 89: The Golf Swing That Took Out My Cousin; A Lesson in Keeping Your Distance 402

Chapter 90: Well, Here We Go Again; My Journey into Fitness Hell 404

Chapter 91: Kora; The Angel Who Saved Zak 409

Chapter 92: How I Swapped a Car That Wasn't Even Mine to Save a Holiday 416

Chapter 93: Stuck in the Door Disaster 422

Chapter 94: The Day the Key Disappeared: A Christmas Comedy of Errors 426

Chapter 95: The Heart That Brought Us Closer; A Story of Love and Gratitude 431

Chapter 96: A New Chapter; The Endless Journey of Life 433

Chapter 97: The Next Adventure Awaits 435

Chapter 98: A Life of Twists, Turns, and Transformations; The Journey of Creation 436

Chapter 99: From the Heart; A Life Lived, A Story Told . 439

Chapter 100: A New Beginning: The Magic of a Life Well Lived 441

About the Author

Geoffrey Loveday, my dad and my children's Papa, is nothing short of extraordinary. He's the calm in every storm—the person we all turn to when life gets tough. But beyond that, he's also one of the most *accident-prone* people on the planet, which makes his life a never-ending series of wild, unbelievable adventures.

Seriously, the stories of his life are the kind that will have you in stitches, crying with laughter, wondering how on earth he's managed to survive it all. That's exactly why I got him to write this book—you won't believe half of what he's been through, and I guarantee you'll be laughing out loud.

My dad is the epitome of resilience and determination. He's faced more challenges than most, and where many would have thrown in the towel, he just kept pushing forward. But the best part? He's done it all with a sense of humour, an endless positivity, and a heart full of compassion.

He doesn't just help people—he *changes* lives, all while somehow managing to trip, stumble, and fall through life's obstacles in the most entertaining ways possible.

His ability to touch lives, combined with his knack for turning everyday situations into hilarious chaos, makes him truly one of a kind.

I am beyond proud to call this inspirational, accident-prone, life-saving whirlwind of a human being my father. After reading this book, you'll not only be in awe of how he's changed lives, but you'll also realise that with Geoffrey Loveday, life is one giant, heart-warming, side-splitting adventure. Buckle up—you're in for a ride!

—Shanna Loveday Davis

Inspiration

This book is a tribute to the extraordinary individuals who have shaped my life and continue to inspire me every day. Their influence, courage, and unwavering support have been instrumental in my journey, and I want to honour them here.

Each day, I am filled with a deep gratitude for the enduring presence my father had in my life—a presence that shaped me in countless ways. Now, in his absence, I feel an indescribable void, a quiet ache that grows with each passing moment, reminding me of his irreplaceable love and guidance.

First and foremost, I dedicate this to the memory of my beloved mother. Though our time together was tragically brief, her spirit remains deeply embedded in my heart. Her absence has taught me to cherish every moment, and her memory continues to guide me with love and strength.

I am equally fortunate to have been nurtured by the profound wisdom and unwavering support of my grandparents, aunts, and uncles. Their lessons, rooted in love and experience, have been a compass on my journey, and their steady encouragement continues to illuminate my path, inspiring me to honour their legacy in all I do.

To my in-laws, Alma and Leon, I extend my heartfelt thanks. Your warm embrace and acceptance into your family have been a gift beyond measure. You have loved me as your own son, and for that, I am eternally grateful."

To my dear wife, whose absence I feel deeply as our children grow, you are forever my guiding light. Your love, strength, and faith in me have been a constant source of motivation, helping me face life's challenges with determination and hope.

To our amazing children, you are my greatest source of joy and inspiration. Your resilience, love, and boundless enthusiasm for life remind me each day of the limitless possibilities that exist, even in the hardest moments. You are living proof of the strength we all carry within us.

To my beautiful grandchildren, your laughter, curiosity, and love for life fill my heart with joy. You are the continuation of our family's legacy, and your presence reminds me of the hope and promise that the future holds.

To my wonderful sons-in-law, who are more like sons to me; your love, respect, and unwavering support have added immeasurable strength to our family. You have embraced our family with open arms, and I am deeply grateful for the bond we share.

I also want to remember my cherished brothers, whose absence has left an irreplaceable void. Your courage and perseverance in the face of hardship inspire me daily. Though we are separated, your memory stays alive in my heart, guiding me with every step.

Lastly, I am deeply thankful to the many friends, mentors, and supporters who have stood by me on this journey. Your guidance, encouragement, and belief in me have been invaluable in bringing this book to life.

To all who have inspired me, whether past or present, this book is dedicated to you. Your impact on my life has been profound, fuelling my passion and shaping my perspective. From the depths of my heart, thank you for everything.

Dedication

To my beautiful and courageous wife...

This book is far more than words on a page; it is a tribute to the extraordinary woman whose love, strength, and spirit touched the hearts of everyone who knew her.

Taken from us far too soon, my wife left a void that can never be filled. Every day, her children and I feel the weight of her absence, a poignant reminder of the incredible person we were blessed to love.

Though the grief of her loss remains, her presence continues to inspire us. She lived with unwavering courage, kindness, and grace, facing every challenge with resilience and embracing life with compassion.

Her boundless heart and strength left an enduring imprint on everyone around her, and her memory continues to guide and uplift us in everything we do.

This book is dedicated to my wife, whose legacy of love and bravery will forever be woven into our lives.

While the pain of losing her may never fully fade, we take comfort in knowing that her radiant spirit still lights our way, especially in life's most difficult moments.

Life doesn't give us a map, only a compass and the courage to keep going.
Geoffrey E Loveday

Chapter 1: The Beginning

When it came to writing my autobiography, the real struggle was: *where on earth do I even start?* How do you pack a lifetime of chaos, catastrophes, and the occasional moment of "wait, did I just do something right?" into one book?

Should I begin with the time I nearly burned down the kitchen while making a cup of tea? (I wasn't even boiling water yet.) Or do I dive headfirst into the wardrobe incident in Wales, where I unintentionally gave a house an extreme makeover by smashing a chandelier and leaving a wardrobe-shaped hole in the ceiling?

Honestly, choosing just one moment is impossible when my life is basically a highlight reel of "you can't make this stuff up" moments. Like the time I literally tripped over my *own shadow*—because apparently, even it's out to get me.

Or the day I locked myself out of my car, called the RAC in full-on panic mode, only to find the keys chilling in my pocket when they showed up. I'm pretty sure even the RAC guy laughed harder than he was supposed to.

So where do I begin? With the accidents? The near-disasters? Or the rare occasions when I actually did something impressive and *nobody was around to see it?* Tough call.

But hey, every story has to start somewhere—so grab a snack, settle in, and get ready to laugh at my misfortune. I promise, if nothing else, it'll make you feel better about your own life!

Life has shown me that it's not the destination that defines us; it's the fire in our hearts, the courage to keep going, and the passion to embrace each new day as if it were our first.

<u>*Geoffrey E Loveday*</u>

Chapter 2: The Real Me

So, after finishing not one, not two, but seven books, my family dropped a bombshell: the book they'd actually be excited to read would be one about...me. Yeah, you heard that right.

Out of everything I've written, they want to know about my life. Naturally, my first thought was, "Who in their right mind would want to read a book about someone who's not famous?"

I mean, in a world where people are devouring celebrity memoirs about how they drink their green smoothies, what hope does my story have?

But then I thought about it some more, and (after several cups of coffee) I realised maybe it's not about being famous.

Maybe it's about the people who matter most—my children. They're the ones I really want to share my journey with. And if anyone else happens to stumble across this book and decides to read it, well, that's just icing on the cake.

So, here it is—an honest, slightly unfiltered look at the rollercoaster ride of my life. The highs, the lows, the times I nailed it, and the times I absolutely didn't.

The lessons I learned (sometimes the hard way) and all the moments that shaped who I am today. This is my story, and you're about to get the behind-the-scenes look. Buckle up!

Chapter 3: This Is My Story, And It's Time to Share It

First off, let me thank you for picking up this book. I'm honestly just as surprised as you are that I'm writing it—well, not just one book, but seven! Yeah, I know, I've got a bit of a habit. But don't worry, this one's different.

This time, I'm telling my real story. Who I am, why I'm here, and why on earth I thought it was a good idea to write this down. You're about to find out that I'm just like you. Yes, we all have a story to tell, and this one? Well, this one's mine.

My name is Geoffrey Elliott Loveday, and I'm a hypnotherapist. For more than forty years, I've worked with people struggling with everything from PTSD to anxiety, OCD, depression, and, well, everything in between. They come to me in pieces—years of therapy, mountains of pills, and programs that haven't quite cracked the code of why they're struggling. That's where I come in with The Loveday Method and Inherited Therapy.

Now, I know what you're thinking: "Wow, Geoffrey, you sound really smart!" I do, don't I? Impressive, right?

But hold on a second. Before you start picturing me as some kind of therapy genius with a PhD in wizardry, let's hit pause. Sure, I've spent years learning, working, and developing methods that sound super important. But let's be real—that's not the whole story.

So, sit back, relax, and let me tell you who I really am. This isn't just about the hypnotherapist version of me. This is the real Geoffrey—the one who laughs at his own jokes, forgets where he put his glasses, and has a whole lot of life stories to share. Buckle up, it's going to be fun!

You've got a glimpse of my life, but let's rewind to the very beginning—way back to the first few awkward pages of my life story. Now, who's this book for? Well, if you're someone who enjoys laughing, crying, feeling the whole emotional rollercoaster—then buckle up, because we're about to go on one heck of a ride together. I promise you won't be disappointed. (And if you are, at least you'll have something to complain about at your next dinner party.)

Hopefully, by the time you reach the end of this book, you'll look back at your own life and say, "Hey, maybe Geoffrey's chaos wasn't so different from mine!"

So, why am I writing this book? Simple. Before I shuffle off this mortal coil, I want to leave behind a little piece of myself.

Something that reminds people who I really was, not just the hypnotherapist or the guy who couldn't find his car keys half the time. We spend so much of life hiding our true selves—but not here, not in these pages. Here, I'm giving you the unfiltered, sometimes awkward, sometimes hilarious, and always honest version of me. Ready? Let's dive in!

Chapter 4: Where It All Started

I was born in Birmingham at Loveday Street Hospital—yes, I know, what are the odds? A Loveday born on Loveday Street, as if my life started with a sense of irony.

I come from a Jewish family and had an incredible, albeit slightly chaotic, childhood. I had two older brothers, Bentley and Morris, who sadly have since passed away. I love them and miss them every day, but boy, did they know how to keep life interesting.

Our house was always filled with laughter, pranks, and the occasional moment where my parents probably questioned their life choices. One particular day stands out: my dad gets a call from a car showroom.

The guy on the other end of the line asks, "Do you have two sons?" My dad, a little confused, says, "Yes..." The seller then informs him that Bentley, my oldest brother, was trying to trade in the younger one—yours truly—for a car. And not just any car, mind you. A Bentley.

I was three at the time. Apparently, Bentley thought the dealership could use a slightly used sibling in exchange for some luxury wheels. And honestly, I'm still not sure if I should be offended or impressed by his negotiation skills!

Summer holidays were always my favourite, mostly because I got to spend them with my amazing grandparents. They were true characters. Both of them came from large families—11 siblings each—and had made their way from Russia to escape the Nazis in the 1940s.

My grandma's family wasn't as fortunate; her siblings and parents were caught and sent to concentration camps. As a child, we never spoke about their suffering—those conversations were strictly off-limits, like a "don't-go-there" zone in our house. We all knew the tragic story, but it was as if talking about it would somehow tear open old wounds.

What they'd said, though, was that once their family members were taken, they were never seen again or heard from again. And this is where my story really begins. From a young age, I used to have recurring nightmares—vivid and terrifying dreams about Nazis and death camps.

Now, these weren't your run-of-the-mill childhood nightmares about monsters under the bed or forgetting your homework. No, these were full-blown night terrors. I'd wake up drenched in sweat, screaming like someone was chasing me.

I began to wonder, even as a child, "Am I reliving someone else's life?" I mean, most children my age were worried about cartoon villains, and here I was practically starring in my own World War II drama every night.

It was like my dreams were less "counting sheep" and more "running from the Gestapo." And let me tell you, no amount of hot chocolate before bed could fix that!

As time went on, the nightmares finally started to fade—thankfully, because let's be honest, waking up in a sweat every night wasn't exactly the beauty sleep I was hoping for.

Still, in the back of my mind, I couldn't help but wonder: why did these nightmares hang around for so long? Was I accidentally living someone else's life? I mean, if I was going to borrow a past life, couldn't it have been someone with fewer Nazis and more naps?

Little did I know, my life's journey was about to serve up the answer, like a plot twist in a movie I didn't know I was starring in.

Chapter 5: My First Grand Entrance

Where do I even begin with my life story? Even though I've been a proud Liverpudlian all my life, half my family—on my mum's side—called Birmingham home.

And let me tell you, my mum was the glue, the matriarch, the one who kept everyone in line. Thanks to her, we basically became a travelling family roadshow: one week, we'd pack up and head down to Birmingham, and the next week, they'd cram into their cars and trek up to Liverpool. We were like a family reunion on tour—same cast, new location, every week.

Now, one fateful week, we're off to Birmingham for the usual family catch-up, when my mum decides to add a plot twist. She goes into labour—two weeks early! No warning, no time to plan, just, "Surprise! Baby's coming whether you're ready or not!"

Her waters break mid-visit, and its absolute chaos. You can imagine—everyone is scrambling, forget tea and biscuits; it's "Find a hospital.

And where does this grand entrance of mine happen? Loveday Street Hospital. You can't make this stuff up! Fate had a field day with this one, practically scripting my life from the start.

So there I am, a curly-headed, red-haired surprise, popping out in Birmingham with a name that sounds straight out of a comedy skit—Geoffrey Elliott Loveday. And yes, I was supposed to be a Liverpudlian, but apparently life had other ideas!

Picture it: my poor mum, expecting a quiet family visit, and instead, she's delivering a baby in a city she didn't even live in. And my first act on this planet? Making a dramatic, surprise appearance in the middle of a family road trip. My family's all gathered around, probably wondering what other plot twists life had up its sleeve.

So, yes, I started life as a Birmingham baby with a Liverpool destiny. If that's not setting the stage for a lifetime of "You won't believe this" moments, I don't know what is. Sometimes, I think my life has been one big punchline since birth, and I've been along for the ride ever since.

So, we finally arrived back home in sunny Liverpool 187 Upper Parliament Street. Now, when I say "home," I mean we lived in my grandfather and grandmother's house... but all of us crammed into one room.

It was a big room, sure, but let's be real—one room is one room! Privacy? Forget it. Space? Hardly. It was a case of "cosy living," and by cosy, I mean we could practically pass each other the salt from bed.

But hey, it was home, and if nothing else, it taught me how to appreciate any personal space I'd get in the years to come!

Chapter 6: My Grandfather, and what I learned following him into the cellar

Life at school and home was nothing short of fascinating—a mix of the everyday and the downright extraordinary. Back then, things were different, and I was surrounded by a world that seemed steeped in history and mystery. My grandfather, for example, was a true character.

He'd fought in World War I and took a bullet straight to the shin. That wound? It never fully healed, leaving a haunting, gaping hole.

I remember following him down into the cellar, watching in awe as he'd sit down, unwind the bandage, and reveal the injury. It was like witnessing history itself, right there in front of me.

But the cellar wasn't just any ordinary storage room; it was practically a museum of wartime relics from both the first and second World Wars. There were bayonets, rifles, and, believe it or not, Japanese swords. The sight of those swords alone would send my imagination spiralling into tales of bravery and far-off battles.

That cellar was like stepping into another world—a place where you felt the weight of history in every corner, from dusty helmets to worn-out uniforms. It was a treasure trove, and I was the lucky kid who got a front-row seat to stories most people only read about in books.

Chapter 7: The day I ran away from my dad: Never again, too much pressure

It's funny, isn't it? When you look back, memories just flood in, one after another. I remember one time when I decided to run away from my dad and ended up completely lost.

I must've been about three and a half, and even at that age, I was a stubborn little thing with a temper to match my red hair. We'd gone shopping across the road from our house on Granby Street, and for reasons I can't even remember, I got upset. I looked at my dad and declared, "I'm not walking there!"

In true "Dad" fashion, he played along, shrugged, and decided to hide. So there I was, huffing and puffing, thinking he'd come back, but after a while, I couldn't find him anywhere. Panic started creeping in. My toddler brain came up with the brilliant idea to walk myself home—I mean, how hard could it be, right?

I knew my grandfather would be home, so I started off, feeling braver than I should have. But don't forget,

I was barely three and a half, and soon enough, I realised I had no idea where the hell I was. The streets seemed massive, and I was just a little red-headed kid, stubbornly stomping along and trying to fight back the tears, wondering how I'd gotten myself into this mess.

I can only imagine the panic that must've hit my dad when he realised I was gone. There he was, playing hide-and-seek with his stubborn little redhead, thinking he had things under control, only to find that I'd actually wandered off. Picture him running around, looking down every aisle, heart pounding, and realising he had to go home and tell my mum that he'd lost me.

The poor guy probably felt worse than I did, imagining the wrath he'd face when he got home. Mum? She would've had his head—no doubt about it. I think that moment was when he realised just how serious my little temper could be!

So, there I was, little legs moving as fast as they could, when I finally spotted my grandfather's house—the one we lived in. Relief washed over me, but there was just one problem: Upper Parliament Street. For a kid barely three and a half, that street might as well have been a six-lane highway.

I'd always been told not to talk to strangers, but desperate times called for desperate measures. I saw this man nearby and called out, "Hey, mister! Can you take me across the road? That's my house over there. I've... lost my dad."

He looked me up and down, probably wondering why a red-headed toddler was handling his own rescue operation, but he took my hand and helped me across. I remember climbing those six massive steps, feeling like I'd reached the end of an epic journey, and knocked on the door. When my grandfather answered, he looked as surprised as if I'd just walked home from the moon.

"Where's your dad?" he asked, eyes wide.

"I've lost him," I managed to say before bursting into tears.

Without missing a beat, he just said, "Go upstairs and hide under the bed." And so I did—my heroic return ending with me tucked under the bed, waiting for the inevitable storm that was about to follow!

Thirty minutes go by, and my dad finally shows up at the front door, looking like he'd just seen a ghost—white as a sheet, eyes wide with worry. He barely gets the words out: "I've lost Geoffrey."

My grandfather, calm as ever, just gives him a nod and says, "He's upstairs under the bed. Be calm; he came home on his own about thirty minutes ago."

My dad's relief must've been mixed with utter disbelief. Thirty minutes of pure panic, only to find out that his "lost" son had already made it home, took matters into his own little hands, and was hiding under the bed, probably clutching the dust bunnies and plotting my next adventure.

I'll bet Dad felt both proud and utterly exasperated—and I had no idea just how many grey hairs I'd probably given him that day!

So there I am, lying under the bed, holding my breath as I hear footsteps coming up the stairs. I'm bracing myself, waiting for all hell to break loose, convinced I'm about to get the scolding of a lifetime.

Then, suddenly, I see my dad's face peeking under the bed. He just looks at me, and instead of the fury I was expecting, he silently points his finger, beckoning me to come out.

I crawl out, half-expecting him to explode, but instead, he pulls me into the biggest hug. I can still feel the tightness of that hug, the relief in it.

I didn't realise until that moment just how much I loved my dad, and maybe, just maybe, how much he loved me too. In his arms, the fear faded, and I knew I was safe.

Chapter 8: The Not-So-Great Ear Adventure: Five Years of Syringes, Needles, and a Bruised Bum

Every weekend, like clockwork, we'd make the drive from Liverpool to Birmingham to visit my mum's sisters and brothers. Family was everything to her, and she was determined to keep everyone connected. Looking back, I realise just how much those visits shaped me, teaching me that family really is important. And it wasn't just us going down; they'd come up to Liverpool as well. It was this constant back-and-forth, a tradition that kept our family bonds strong.

But then, something strange started happening to me. Every time we made that drive to Birmingham, I'd get this unbearable earache. I was only six, but the pain was enough to bring me to tears. Mum or Dad would have to rock me to sleep just to calm me down. Once we'd get back home in Liverpool, it was straight to the doctor, and another round of antibiotics to keep the pain at bay. The earache would ease up, only to come roaring back the next time we headed to Birmingham. This became a regular pattern: trip to Birmingham, earache, trip to the doctor. Over and over.

For years, I had no idea why it kept happening. But many years later, I finally found out why.

My mum and dad finally realised that something was definitely wrong, so they booked me an appointment with a specialist. Now, in my world, "What could possibly go wrong?" usually meant "What fresh chaos is about to unfold?" And sure enough, it turned out I was in for a two-week hospital stay and an operation. Apparently, if I didn't have it, I'd lose the hearing in my right ear. Lovely news, right? But back then, nobody explained things to kids, so I had no idea what was going on. I was six, after all—barely out of the "building blocks" stage of brain development.

Then came the big day, and they took me to the hospital. Now, you have to understand, this was one of those ancient hospitals that looked like it was straight out of Florence Nightingale's era. Dark hallways, old wooden floors, the kind of place that could make you feel creepy even in daylight. And here I was, this little kid, about to face whatever strange adventure awaited me inside that building. Little did I know, the fun was just beginning!

The hospital was run by this matron who could've easily doubled as a drill sergeant. She had this way about her—stern, efficient, and with a gaze that could freeze you in place. It was like she was running an army camp, and every nurse and patient seemed absolutely petrified of her. No talking back, no slouching, and certainly no sneaking out of bed for a midnight snack. Things were about to change, and in my little six-year-old mind, I was about to face the toughest "commanding officer" I'd ever met.

When I first arrived, I genuinely believed my mum and dad would be able to stay with me. I didn't realise that back then, visiting hours were the only times you could see family. The reality hit hard as soon as they left, and for the first time, I felt this deep, aching loneliness. That night, as I lay there in the unfamiliar bed, the silence was deafening. I remember curling up under the scratchy hospital blanket, tears rolling down my face as I tried to hide how scared I felt. I wanted to go home, to be anywhere but there.

It was a horrible feeling for a little boy, a sadness that felt almost too big to carry. I had two whole weeks in that place, where everything felt cold, strange, and lonely. Looking back, that was the first time I truly understood what it felt like to be alone, and it left a mark that I still remember.

Eventually, I sort of came to terms with my "sentence." They told me it'd be two weeks, though, at six years old, I had no idea what two weeks even meant. For all I knew, I'd be in there forever—or at least until I grew a beard like my dad's!

So there I was, trying to grasp the concept of time, thinking, "Well, two weeks... sounds short... or maybe long?" Honestly, I was just hoping they'd let me out before I turned 18.

When my family came to visit, it was like a breath of fresh air in that place. But when they left, the sadness would just settle in like a thick blanket, making that quiet hospital feel even bigger and emptier. I remember watching them disappear down the hall, holding back the urge to sprint after them. I felt so small, left in this vast, silent world of bandages and beeping machines.

To distract myself from the loneliness—and let's be real, to keep from going completely mad—I got up to all kinds of mischief. The matron? Oh, she was my nemesis. She ran the place like it was boot camp, and I quickly became her top recruit in the "rule-breaker's division." Every time she thought she had me under control, I'd find a new way to cause some small disaster. I mean, what was I supposed to do—stare at the walls all day?

But slowly, I somehow started to break down her icy exterior. After one especially "energetic" game of hide-and-seek with the other patients, we reached a truce. I promised to keep my antics to a minimum if she agreed to ease up on the terrifying glare and endless "tsk-tsks." It became our little pact—she'd stop acting like a prison guard if I stopped treating the place like an amusement park. Shockingly, it worked.

By the time my operation was looming, I'd managed to turn the matron from "Drill Sergeant" to "Mildly Tolerant Neighbour." She was almost friendly... almost.

I don't remember much about the operation itself—just a blur of doctors, bright lights, and probably some odd smells. But it must've gone well because soon enough, my family came to take me home. And just before we left, the matron—the same woman who'd been terrifying me for weeks—swooped down and gave me this enormous hug, nearly squeezing the life out of me. I must've looked like a deer in headlights, and thinking, "Is this a trap?" I'd been trying to dodge her wrath for so long, I didn't know how to handle a hug from her.

But the best part was finally heading home, escaping that place of soggy toast and jam every morning. Ah, yes—the breakfast specialty that only hospitals can perfect: toast that was somehow both too damp and too crunchy at the same time, with a slathering of jam that looked more medicinal than fruity. I swear, I can still smell it if I think about it too hard!

But it didn't end there. A few weeks later, I had to go back to see the doctor for the results, and of course, my whole family came along—after all, I was only six! The doctor gave me the good news: everything had gone well, and my ear was in good shape. But then came the catch. He said I'd need to return to the hospital to have my ear "syringed."

Now, no one had explained what that meant, so I just imagined some machine with whirring parts and a giant red light, spinning around inside my head. I could feel my heart racing, picturing it like a scene from a sci-fi horror movie.

Oh, I wasn't far off in my sci-fi horror movie vision! They brought out this contraption that looked like a massive syringe with a weird red goo at the end, practically glowing. They stuck it in my ear, and at first, it just tickled a bit, and I thought, "Hey, maybe this won't be so bad."

Then it started spinning like a tiny washing machine in my head! Tickling turned to awful buzzing, and just when I thought it was over, they whipped out this needle—and not one of those dainty ones like they have now. No, this was a colossal thing, practically a harpoon, and where does it go? Right in my bum!

And just when I thought I'd seen the last of it, the doctor tells me, "Oh, by the way, you'll need to come in for this every day for the next five years." Five years! I was a walking pin cushion, already dreading the next time. Every day, right on schedule, I'd trudge back with my dad, both of us bracing for round two, three, and four—me holding onto my dignity, one syringe spin at a time.

Many years later, I finally figured out why I was always getting ear aches as a kid. Turns out, the mystery culprit was right under my nose—or rather, right under my nose in a cloud of smoke. My parents, bless them, had no idea that every time they lit up a cigarette in the car, they were unknowingly torturing my poor little ears. They'd be puffing away, windows barely cracked, while I sat in the backseat, slowly turning into a human smoke detector.

They had no clue their smoking sessions were causing me so much pain. Every car ride felt like my ears were in a boxing match, and meanwhile, they'd be up front, happily chain-smoking and wondering why their kid always ended up at the doctor's. It is funny, looking back... in a tragic, ear-aching sort of way!

Chapter 9: The Day I Tried to Fly... through a Glass Door

The first years of my life were interesting, to say the least. We didn't have much—no TV, no washing machine. Entertainment? Well, that was mostly looking at the pictures in books and finding creative ways to survive our own household adventures.

Now, keep in mind, this was no modern house. We're talking late 1800s construction, complete with two massive double glass doors leading to the front entryway. No safety glass back then, just thick, old-school glass waiting for an accident. And believe me, it got one.

So here's the scene: we didn't have a washing machine or dryer, so the clothes would be wrapped up in a sheet, the corners tied together like a big laundry bundle, and taken downstairs to be picked up by a van. Simple task, right? What could possibly go wrong? (Yeah, I really need to stop saying that.)

My brother Bentley was told to take this massive bundle of clothes downstairs, and for whatever reason, I decided to "help" by grabbing onto it, even though I was more like extra luggage than actual help. Bentley's hauling it down, I'm hanging on like a little sidekick, and we're approaching those giant double glass doors. One door is open, the other door—well, it's closed.

Now, Bentley, the smart one, steers right through the open door. Me? I don't let go in time, and I go sailing straight through the closed glass door like Superman, only with less grace and more glass shattering everywhere. I crash through, hit the front door, and my head splits open, blood everywhere. It must have looked like a horror movie.

My poor grandmother? She screams, "You've killed him!" like it's already over. I don't remember much after that because, well... I passed out. But one thing's for sure: it was a day no one forgot. And me? I'd gotten my first real taste of "What could possibly go wrong?"

Trust me; that was just the beginning. If you think that was the worst of it, you clearly haven't been following along. That little flight through the glass door?

Just the opening act. Because with my luck, the universe was only warming up. Turns out, "What could possibly go wrong?" would become a regular event, each one bigger and messier than the last.

And if you think my grandmother was shocked that day, just wait till you hear what happened next...

Chapter 10: The Day I Picked a Fight with a Brick Wall (and Lost)

Back then, there was no fancy nursery—you were five, you went into infants, and that was that. Imagine it: the place looked straight out of Tom Brown's School Days or some old Charles Dickens novel. It was like stepping back in time, where everything creaked and the head teacher probably owned a collection of antique canes. For a five-year-old, it was borderline terrifying. But hey, you adjusted... eventually. School ran from 9:15 a.m. to 4:30 p.m., which felt like an eternity. For a little kid, it was like pulling a full shift at the factory!

And if you thought mornings went smoothly, think again—I was always late. And let me tell you, they took punctuality seriously. Being late meant a one-way ticket to the humiliation station, right there in front of the whole school during assembly. The teachers had real power back then, armed with a slipper, a ruler, their hand, and the dreaded cane. Infants weren't too bad, but in junior you'd better keep your head down.

Every morning, I'd be on edge, wondering if I'd make it on time. More often than not, I didn't, so I had my little routine: arrive late, sneak off to hide in the toilets, and hope they'd forget about me. But they always found me. I'd get dragged to assembly, where I'd stand up there, feeling like a criminal on display.

And this didn't happen just once or twice—no, I became a regular in the "late arrival" line-up. So, I finally made some friends—my best mates, Colin Williams and Ian Hart.

Colin was a bit of a troublemaker, and he had me running into mischief left and right. The kid was unstoppable, and I'll admit, we had the time of our lives.

Then there was Ian, who was just as funny but had this knack for getting me into trouble without lifting a finger. Now, these two shot up like weeds, while I stayed the "compact" one of the group. And did I mention I was a redhead? Because, naturally, with the hair came the temper.

One day, Ian was just being a complete pain. It was during one of those endless 30-minute breaks out in the yard. And, as usual, he was towering over me, poking fun and pushing my last button. I could feel my blood boiling, I was fuming, so I decided to do the reasonable thing and smack him in the face—classic, right?

While he was chatting to someone, at the very last second, he moved out of the way oblivious to what was happening. My punch sailed past him and went full speed into the jagged brick wall behind him.

That's right—I punched a wall. My hand exploded in pain, and in seconds I was clutching it like my life depended on it. Turns out, I'd broken my wrist and four fingers in my "act of bravery." But did I tell Ian what I'd actually tried to do? Not a chance.

The embarrassment would've been worse than the pain. Ian saw me cradling my hand and, being the good friend he was, assumed I'd slipped, so he walked me to the nurse.

She asked what happened, and I spun this story about losing my balance on the asphalt. I think even she knew I was lying, but she played along.

And Ian? He had no idea I'd aimed that punch at him! To this day, he never found out I'd tried to deck him but ended up in a fistfight with a wall instead. I think the guilt was almost as bad as the pain, but not quite enough to admit the truth!

Chapter 11: Learning My Lesson: You Think? No Way

After that glass-door fiasco and breaking my wrist and fingers, you'd think I might have learned my lesson. But no—far from it. That was just the beginning of a long series of "character-building" incidents where, naturally, I was the star of my own disasters. Take Mrs. Birch, for example. She had me pegged as trouble from day one, and let's just say, I lived up to her expectations in ways that still make me laugh—and cringe—a little.

It seemed like everywhere I went, I found a new way to turn an ordinary day into a spectacle. I was like a magnet for mishaps, and if there was a way to accidentally cause chaos, you could bet I'd find it. If there's one thing life taught me early on, it's that trouble doesn't need an invitation. In my case, it just showed up, followed me around, and occasionally dragged me through a glass door for good measure.

Chapter 12: The Day I Outsmarted Mrs. Birch... Kind Of

Talking about Mrs Birch she really had me pegged.

Ah, Mrs. Birch's class in J2—what a horror show that was! She was tiny but ran her classroom like a drill sergeant, and, let's just say, I was not her favourite. I was a chatterbox, always talking when I shouldn't, especially in the last lesson before home time. And there I was, sitting in my classic grey school shorts, chatting away with this girl next to me, thinking I'd gotten away with it.

Suddenly, out of the corner of my eye, I see Mrs. Birch marching over, eyes narrowed. Before I knew it, she grabbed me by the scruff of my neck and yanked me up onto the chair. "Stand up!" she barked, and I didn't even have time to think before she started whacking the back of my thigh. Not once, not twice—but seven times!

And let me tell you, these weren't little love taps. No, it was like she was trying to tune my leg like a drum, and the pain was something out of this world. I could feel my eyes welling up, but I was determined not to let her see me cry.

Then, right in the middle of the pin-drop silence in the classroom, I blurted out, "Well, that was fun!"

The whole class lost it, absolutely roaring with laughter. Mrs. Birch went bright red and shrieked, "Sit down or you're off to Mr. Nagly for the cane!" Now, I might've been cheeky, but I wasn't an idiot—I sat down so fast you'd have thought the chair was made of gold.

Chapter 13: Happy Times: My Unforgettable Childhood

Life from early childhood was full of unusual experiences, to say the least! My family all smoked like chimneys. I remember staring at the kitchen walls, thinking they were painted this lovely golden yellow— only to realise, later on, it was nicotine.

Can you believe it? Everyone in my family smoked, but me? I never touched a cigarette or even a drink. I know, I'm the odd one out! And if my dad ever caught me smoking... let's just say I'd probably still be hearing about it today!

Growing up as a kid was a blast. Every night felt like an episode of The Waltons. We'd do our nightly "I love you"— "Love you, Mum!" "Love you, Dad!" "Love you, Ben!" And on and on until my brother would finally shout, "For the love of all things, PLEASE be quiet!" ... though he might have phrased it a little differently.

Christmas was pure magic. Mum and Dad made sure of it. I'd be so excited the night before, I'd hardly sleep.

And then in the morning, there it was—a massive black bin bag stuffed with presents, waiting just for me. I can still remember tearing into it, finding treasures inside like a tangerine, a box of Christmas chocolates, model planes to build, Monopoly, The Broons, Dandy, and Beano books—each gift was a world of fun. Life was so simple then, and I appreciated every single bit of it.

We'd play card games, and I was obsessed with magic tricks. Those were the days—full of family, fun, and a little chaos, but I wouldn't trade them for the world.

Chapter 14: From Parliament Street to Paradise: Moving to Gateacre Park Drive

When I was ten, we moved from Upper Parliament Street to a brand-new house at 5 Gateacre Park Drive in Childwall. It was just built, and stepping into that place felt like stepping into a whole new world.

I had my own bedroom—my own room!—and every room even had its own electric fire built right into the wall. It was pure heaven, honestly. It was like we'd moved to the countryside; everything was green and peaceful, such a difference from the busy streets of our old neighbourhood.

I remember that first morning waking up, with the sun streaming in through the window. I could hear birds singing, and everything felt fresh and alive. After all of us crammed into one room, this felt like pure freedom.

Everything was new—the carpets, the walls, even the smell. I don't think I'll ever forget that feeling. It was a moment of pure magic for a ten-year-old boy.

We had so much fun in that house—plenty of laughter, a few tears, but mostly happy times. Even though our time there was shorter than I would have liked (as you'll soon find out), it was a magical place filled with memories.

Chapter 15: A New Adventure at King David High: Football Dreams, Hebrew Drills, and the First Crush

It was time for the next big step: high school. I remember my first day, feeling that mix of excitement and nervousness. My brother had just left King David High School, and he was practically a legend there—everyone knew and liked him. No pressure, right?

Weeks went by, and I quickly learned that high school days were long—really long. We'd start at 9:00 a.m. and not finish until 4:30 p.m., and just when I thought I'd get a break, it was straight off to chaider (Hebrew school) from 5:00 till 6:00.

Except on Fridays, thank goodness—that was the one day of freedom, no Hebrew drills. And let's be honest, it wasn't exactly by choice. I was made to go, no ifs, ands, or buts about it.

That first day was all about figuring out the lay of the land, meeting the teachers, and quickly learning which ones to avoid. Fortunately, the day went off without a hitch, and in the weeks that followed, I started making friends, playing football, and finding my way in this whole new world. It felt like the beginning of something big, and I was ready for the adventure.

It was at a Jewish school—Jewish and non-Jewish kids together—where academics were amazing, or so they said.

All I wanted to do was play football, but that didn't always line up with their grand educational plan. One day, though, something happened that took my mind right off football.

Chapter 16: The day I fell in love, I was only ten

It was a beautiful summer's day, and I was in the middle of a French lesson. The room was stuffy, my attention was somewhere between the chalkboard and the window, when suddenly, I noticed the girl sitting in front of me.

She was... beautiful. I don't know what came over me, but that day, in that moment, I fell head-over-heels in love. Don't laugh—it's true! I was only ten, but it felt so real, like I'd been hit by some cosmic force. I had never felt anything like it in my entire life.

Naturally, I had to know her name, so I asked a friend on the sly. That night, I went to sleep and had the most incredible dreams about her—dreams so good that I actually didn't want to wake up.

This feeling wasn't normal. It wasn't even from this world. It was like I'd known her from somewhere before, like she was my soulmate from another lifetime. Sounds dramatic, right? But in my ten-year-old heart, it was as real as anything.

Her name was Sharon, and once I found that out, I had to ask her out. Naturally, I told my friends, who looked at me like I'd lost my mind. And maybe they were right.

Every time I worked up the nerve to ask her, she'd be surrounded by these two "bodyguard" friends, like they knew exactly what I was up to. I'd inch closer, heart pounding, and just as I was about to say something, they'd link arms and trot off, leaving me in the dust. It was like some perfectly orchestrated escape plan!

But one day, I finally had her cornered—no escape routes, no friends. I took a deep breath, stammered out my question, and she said... yes! I couldn't believe it. I felt like I'd won the World Cup, right there in the middle of the playground.

But, of course, with me, there's always a catch. I learned that very quickly in life. Turns out, I had to call up her father and ask permission to take her out.

Let me repeat that: I was ten years old, dialling up her dad like some mini Romeo, asking if I could "take his daughter out." I should've been on the field playing football, not managing love affairs and parental permissions!

I remember it like it was yesterday: it was a Saturday, and I was supposed to call Sharon's dad to ask if I could take his daughter out. I mean, I was ten years old, for goodness' sake! My heart was pounding as I picked up the phone. I dialled, and after what felt like a century, someone finally answered.

"Who is this?" he barks.

And in my head, I'm thinking, "It's Noddy! Who do you think it is?" Because, apparently, when you're ten and absolutely terrified, your brain just flips to cartoon characters.

Silence. Then, "Geoffrey, isn't it?"

"Y-yes, sir…" I stammered, suddenly regretting every life choice that led to this moment.

"So, I hear you want to take my daughter out." He pauses. "What are your intentions?"

Intentions? I'm ten! What intentions could I possibly have, other than maybe sharing my lunch and maybe, maybe holding her hand if I was feeling particularly daring? But I'm frozen, so I just squeak out, "Uh... good ones?"

He sighs, probably holding back laughter. "Good intentions, huh?"

"Yes, sir! Only the goodest, sir!"

More silence. Then, in this super serious dad voice, he finally says, "Alright, Geoffrey. But I'll be watching you."

I nearly dropped the phone. I hung up, feeling like I'd just gone through boot camp, all so I could maybe take Sharon to play on the swings!

So, I finally talked to her at school, and—yep—the feelings were still very much there. We arranged to meet up that Thursday at Harold House, the Jewish youth club in Liverpool where I usually went for five-a-side football.

Thursday rolls around, and I'm practically bouncing off the walls. I mean, it's Harold House—a place I usually went to for a good kick about with the lads. But tonight, football was taking a back seat because I had a date. Well, a ten-year-old's version of a date.

So, we met up that night, and I was buzzing—thinking this was going to be the stuff of legends. We snuck around to the back of the club for a kiss and a cuddle, and in my head, I'm expecting fireworks, angels singing, maybe even the heavens opening up. But you know what? Nothing. No sparks, no choirs, just... meh.

I stood there, a bit disappointed, thinking, "Well, that was anticlimactic." So, I did the only sensible thing: I shrugged, said, "See ya," and went straight back to play five-a-side football. And that, ladies and gents, was the end of my love life—for a while, anyway.

Chapter 17: The Night I Traded Milk for Whiskey, and Paid the Price (With a Broken Nose)

When I was about 17, Graham and I went out to a club in town called Uglies, in Duke Street in Liverpool. Now, a group of us would meet up there regularly, the plan being to impress the girls (or at least give it a shot).

I should probably mention—I don't drink. I never have. In fact, every time I went to the bar, I'd confidently ask for a glass of milk. At first, they laughed, but eventually, they got used to it and started having a glass ready for me.

One night, my mate Martin decides to go after my "milk-drinker" reputation. "You couldn't handle a real drink if your life depended on it!" he says, in front of everyone.

Now, I'm not one to back down from a challenge, so I said, "Of course I can drink. I just choose not to." Martin grins and says, "Alright, then. I bet you fifty pounds you can't down three double whiskies." Fifty quid! That was five weeks of my wages. But before I could think it through, everyone was watching, egging me on, and next thing I knew, I'd accepted.

"Fine. You're on. But you're buying the drinks."

So there I am, standing in front of three double whiskies, with half the club watching like it's the event of the century. Three doubles... How hard can it be? I think.

First one down—it burns like the pits of hell, but I keep a straight face. Martin shoves the second one at me, practically grinning. I'm sweating a bit now, but I throw it back. Finally, I'm on to the third, take a deep breath, and down it like a champion.

I hand him the empty glass, and in the coolest voice I can manage, I say, "Alright, Martin, fifty pounds, please." Martin looks at me, smirking, and says, "You know I'm good for it, mate." And you know what? I thought I'd won. I felt fine. Brilliant, even.

Then it's time to go home. I swagger to the club's front door, head held high, and the bouncer opens it. The second that fresh air hits me, I'm done. My knees buckle, and I go down like a sack of bricks, rolling down five steps and landing at the bottom with a broken bloody nose.

By the way I ended up in hospital that night, and woke up the next day with two black eyes.

And that's how I learned the hard way that some bets are just not worth fifty quid.

Chapter 18: The Quiet Strength of a Mother's Love: A Journey through Faith, Fear, and Unspoken Battles

This is a story that must be told, a story of love, of fate, and of unimaginable tragedy. This is why my mother's cancer returned. But to understand, we need to go back — back to a sun-drenched summer in 1965, a time when life seemed limitless, when my mother was young, full of dreams, and unaware of the darkness that would eventually find her.

I was almost fourteen, teetering on the edge of childhood, looking out at a world that felt thrilling and safe. My mother and her friend had booked a holiday in Israel, and her excitement was contagious.

It was a trip we were supposed to cherish forever, a two-week escape into warmth, history, and laughter. But life rarely turns out as we expect, and as I grew older, I came to believe that everything happens for a reason — even when that reason breaks your heart.

We explored and wandered, our days filled with sun-drenched excursions and the chatter of newfound friends. I remember one day in particular, an excursion to a place so deeply woven into the stories of ancient faith — Mount Ararat, the legendary resting place of Noah's Ark. Its towering presence, the weight of its myth, felt almost alive.

And yet, amid the laughter and awe, an invisible thread was being woven, binding us to something larger, something terrifying. Looking back now, I know that what happened on that trip would alter the course of our lives forever, shaping everything that followed.

That moment — the one that stays with me, that I will carry in my heart to the very end — is a truth I wish I could forget. And yet, it's one I have to share.

Because this is the story of why my mother's cancer came back. And this is just the beginning.

So there we were, on an excursion to a place woven deeply into the fabric of ancient faith — Mount Ararat, where legends say Noah's Ark came to rest. The mountain loomed above us, a place of quiet power and solemn beauty. As we stood there, gazing down at the rough stones scattered along the path, life felt both vast and strangely close, like the world had folded in on this one sacred moment.

But then it happened. My mother, standing just a few steps ahead, lost her footing. I watched in horror as she slipped, her body suddenly sliding down the jagged mountain path, her face contorted in a mix of shock and pain.

We ran down after her, our hearts pounding with every step, the world around us a blur. I remember the way the stones sounded under our feet, sharp and unforgiving.

When we reached her, she was lying still, her leg twisted unnaturally. I didn't know what to do, and the silence around us felt endless, broken only by her shallow breaths.

An ambulance arrived sooner than I could have imagined, and they took her to a nearby hospital. The drive was a haze of fear and waiting, the hours folding in on themselves until we heard the news: she had broken her leg. The doctors set it in plaster, her leg immobilised, her spirit quiet and steady.

A few days later, they arranged for a flight back home to Liverpool. She was in pain — I could see it in the lines etched on her face, though she never said a word. My mother was always strong, always trying to shield me from the heaviness of her suffering.

Finally, we landed back in Liverpool, and as we stepped through the door, a wave of relief and sorrow hit me so hard I could barely breathe. All the fear, all the worry I'd been holding back came rushing out.

I broke down in tears, clinging to her as I realised how deeply it had affected me. I hadn't let myself feel it until then, hadn't understood how much seeing her in pain had hollowed out some part of me. And I thought, maybe, that we had left it all behind on that mountain.

But as life would soon show us, some things never stay behind.

What I haven't yet told you is that my mother had breast cancer, something I didn't know at the time, though she had been in remission. She was quiet about her illness, protective as always, trying to keep the weight of her struggle hidden from me.

But now, looking back, I feel certain that the shock of that fall — that brutal tumble down the unforgiving stones of Mount Ararat — might have been the moment something shifted within her.

Her leg healed, but as time went on, I could sense that something wasn't right. I wasn't told much, but a bed was moved downstairs, and I stayed by her side, ready to help however I could. My young heart beat with worry I didn't yet know how to voice. I watched her, day after day, trying to read the expression on her face, trying to understand the unspoken pain that lingered between us.

Then, that same year, the world around us grew even darker. In 1967, Israel came under attack — a conflict that would become known as the Six-Day War.

My older brother, full of idealism and strength, decided to volunteer on a kibbutz with his friends, determined to help however he could. For six long months, he was out there, thousands of miles away, in a country caught in a storm of violence and uncertainty.

I think of my mother then, bearing not just the physical scars of her fall but the silent wounds of a mother's worry. I know now that she must have spent countless nights awake, wondering if she'd see her son again, fearing for his life.

I wonder, even to this day, if that worry and fear somehow pulled her back into the darkness she thought she'd escaped. Was it the shock of her fall? The stress of her son's departure? I'll never truly know, and the questions still haunt me.

But what I do know is this: she faced it all with quiet strength, bearing her pain without complaint, holding us close to her heart as her own began to falter. And that strength — her unwavering, resilient love — is something I carry with me every day, a reminder of what she endured and the light she left behind.

Not long after, my mum passed away at home. I remember the moment with an aching clarity — my dad coming upstairs, his face hollow, eyes cast down, as he told me.

The words seemed to echo in the room, filling it with a silence heavier than anything I had known. I couldn't understand why this had happened. She was the heart of our family, my anchor, the one who held everything together.

The sadness that flooded me was overwhelming, a weight that seemed to press down on my chest, making it hard to breathe. It was as if the world had shifted, like the very ground beneath my feet was pulled away. And in that single, shattering moment, everything changed.

Life was never the same after that. She left behind a silence that settled into every corner of our home, a reminder of her absence that I felt each day. I was left with memories, questions, and a grief that would become a part of me — shaping who I was and who I would become.

Chapter 19: The day my world was turned upside down

At 14 years old, my world was turned upside down. My mum was diagnosed with breast cancer, and not long after, she passed away. She wasn't just my mum—she was the rock of our family, the matriarch who held everything together. When she died, it felt like everything I knew, everything I relied on, was taken from me in an instant. A part of my dad died with her, too.

It wasn't long before my dad met someone else, and from that moment, I knew things would never be the same again. School became a burden, and the joy and laughter that once defined me and my brothers were replaced by a deep, painful sadness. Then, one night, I came home to see my suitcase, packed and sitting in the hallway. My dad told me I'd be staying at my auntie's for a few weeks.

That was the moment I realised my home—my safe space—was being taken away.

I remember walking into my aunt's house with trepidation, feeling like an outsider, like I didn't belong. My aunt and uncle never made me feel unwelcome—this was all in my head—but I couldn't shake the feeling that I was a guest in their home, not a part of it. The memory of standing in their living room, clutching my suitcase, wishing desperately to be back home, is something that has stayed with me ever since.

Their home was nothing like mine. There was no heating, and they were strict—something I wasn't used to at all. I went from a house full of warmth and laughter to a house full of cold silence. My father wasn't there. My brothers weren't there. I felt like a lost little boy, left to fend for myself emotionally.

To be fair, my aunt and uncle were kind, caring people. They fed me, clothed me, gave me a roof over my head—but it never felt like home. Every day, I convinced myself, "This won't last long. I'll be back home soon." But deep down, I always knew that wasn't true. Sometimes, we don't want to face the truth. We run from it, hoping that if we don't acknowledge it, it won't become real.

Looking back, I realise how naïve I was. I wish I could go back and speak to my younger self, reassure him, tell him that everything would be okay eventually. That's all I needed at the time—someone to say, "Geoff, it's going to be alright." But that reassurance never came.

Looking back at my life, I sometimes think the universe had a funny way of trying to cheer me up. Like it saw all the sadness I went through when I was younger and thought, "You know what? Let's throw him a bunch of ridiculous catastrophes to lighten things up. That should help!" Maybe all those disasters were the universe's way of saying, "Forget the sadness—let's give you some unbelievable stories, even though you won't know how you survived them."

It's like every time I got too comfortable, the universe whispered, "Not today, Geoff!" and suddenly I'd be knee-deep in some absurd disaster that nobody else would believe unless they saw it with their own eyes. Honestly, it's like life's been one long comedy sketch, where I'm the punchline and the audience just keeps laughing.

But you know what? Maybe that was the plan all along. How can you dwell on the past when you're busy explaining to someone how you accidentally set off a chain reaction of catastrophes? Maybe the universe figured, "Let's give him a life so full of madness that he can't help but laugh at it all—eventually, anyway."

Weeks turned into months, and months turned into years. During that time, everything in my life unravelled. My dad remarried, our family home—the place that held all my childhood memories—was sold. And with it, every piece of my past seemed to disappear. Everything I once clung to for comfort and familiarity was gone. My childhood possessions, the things I thought I'd hold onto forever, were discarded, lost like they never mattered.

I loved comics—Superman especially. I spent hours in my room, escaping into those stories, where the world made sense, and heroes always saved the day. Those comics were more than just books to me—they were my refuge. But they, too, were tossed out, like they were just clutter, like they hadn't been the only thing that gave me solace in those dark moments. I can still feel the ache of that loss, the emptiness that came when everything familiar was ripped away.

At the time, it felt like the universe was playing a cruel game, taking away everything that anchored me. It was more than just losing things; it felt like losing myself. But now, after all these years, I've come to realise something. Life has a way of breaking you down just to build you back up. Every painful moment, every loss, was part of a process I didn't understand at the time. It was shaping me, forcing me to grow, even though it felt unbearable.

I couldn't see it then, but now I know—those moments of heartbreak, of feeling completely lost, were meant to happen. They're what made me who I am today. And while it hurt deeply, I wouldn't be this person without all of it.

It's strange, looking back. The memories I thought I'd buried so deeply—the ones I thought I'd locked away for good—have suddenly come flooding back. And now, as I sit here writing, the tears are flowing down my face, unstoppable, like a dam finally breaking. I never realised just how much sadness was still sitting there, waiting to come up to the surface. It's as if all those years, I had been trying so hard to forget, thinking if I buried them deep enough, they couldn't hurt me again.

But now, I can't stop it. The tears, the grief, the ache of those memories—they all come rushing back as if I'm living it all over again. I thought I'd moved past it, that by shoving it down and not talking about it, I could protect myself. But now, I see I was only delaying the inevitable. It's like all the pain I tried to hide is demanding to be felt, reminding me that some wounds never fully heal.

And here I am, sitting with tears running down my face, realising just how deeply those moments still affect me. It's funny how life works—you think you've outrun the pain, but it always finds a way to catch up with you.

Chapter 20: A sadness that cut deep

There are moments in life that cut deep, leaving marks that never fully fade. Living at my auntie's was one of those times. In the beginning, it was unbelievably hard—trying to adjust to a new way of life, surrounded by familiar faces but feeling like a stranger in a world that wasn't my own. Each day felt heavy, like I was carrying the weight of everything I'd lost.

But as the years passed, slowly, I began to find my footing. The tears, once so constant, started to fade. In their place, little by little, came moments of peace and even laughter. I found myself smiling again, learning that while some scars never fully heal, life somehow gives you reasons to smile again. And those moments, however small, helped me see that maybe—just maybe—there was light on the other side.

As I mentioned, I used to work for my brother Morris. That life was never really meant for me, though, and deep down, I always sensed I was meant for something greater. It sounds strange now, saying that, but my brother believed it too. When our mum passed, he took it incredibly hard. I think he felt her presence guiding him, urging him to push me toward a better future, one beyond what we knew. I miss him more than I can express; he wanted so much more for me, even when I couldn't see it myself.

At that time, I didn't feel like I had much of a future. I felt like an outsider, unsure of where I belonged, or even if anyone really cared. Losing Mum only deepened that feeling, and at just 15, I thought I could help Dad somehow. He was struggling with so much—financially, emotionally—and I thought maybe I could make things easier for him. So I left school, barely scraping by on my GCSEs, and threw myself into whatever work I could find. I wanted to help him, to fill a void I didn't understand but felt deeply.

Looking back, I can see the people who were there for me, those who saw potential in me when I couldn't see it myself. And for them, I am truly grateful. In those early years, I was searching for a way to make sense of a world without my mum, a world where I felt like I had to step up, even when I wasn't ready. Every step I took was in hopes of helping, of honouring her, of finding my place.

I went from one job to another in those early days, finding my footing and figuring out who I was along the way. I remember my first real job at Henderson's in Liverpool, where I was training to be a buyer. I earned a humble £9.99 a week, but to me, it felt like a start. It was there that I met seven lads from Kirkby. At first, we were strangers, but in time, they became close friends. They taught me something I didn't realise I was searching for: friendship and belonging.

There's always one in every group who holds the sway, and in ours, that was Michael. He was 6'2", towering over my 5'8" frame, and he had the confidence of a leader. Being Jewish, I wore my Star of David with pride, even in a time and place where antisemitism was still all too common. I learned early that sometimes you need to face things head-on, so I decided to have a straightforward talk with Michael. I looked him in the eye and said, "I'm Jewish. If you've got a problem with that, we'd best sort it out now."

He paused, and in that moment, something shifted. From that day forward, he had a newfound respect for me, and the subject never came up again. There was a mutual understanding, an unspoken bond that we all shared, and it made our friendship stronger.

Those days, and those friendships, became a foundation for me. We shared countless adventures, navigating life and finding ourselves along the way. It was then I realised that sometimes, the friends you make in unexpected places can become the family you never saw coming. And in their own way, they helped me grow into the person I wanted to be.

I've never been one for working under someone else—I think it's in the blood. With a family full of self-employed go-getters, punching someone else's clock just didn't sit right with me.

I was living at my auntie's at the time, catching up with my dad here and there, and he must've sensed my restlessness. One day, he had a chat with my brother Bentley and convinced him to give me a shot on the markets. I was thrilled! Bentley, though? Not so much.

So there I was, selling records—the good, old-fashioned vinyl ones that weighed a ton. In the summer, it was fantastic! Music, sunshine, crowds… especially the girls, who seemed to love flipping through records.

But winter? You've got to be kidding! Between the cold winds and trying to keep those vinyl records from warping, it was character-building to say the least. My record-selling career may have been short-lived, but it was an experience I'll never forget.

Then I started working for Morris. Now, working for Morris was its own education. We were having one of our usual chats, and he started telling me his father-in-law had a friend who was a diamond cutter and was looking to pass on his skills before retiring.

A diamond cutter! I was practically vibrating with excitement at the thought—I mean, diamonds! Training to be a jeweller! I could already picture myself, tools in hand, working with the finest stones.

But then, just as quickly as my dreams had sparkled, they shattered. Morris mentioned, oh-so-casually, "Yeah… but then the diamond cutter passed away. Sad, really."

My excitement dropped like a brick. There I was, ready to set off on a glamorous new career, and it was over before it even began!

So, after my brother had experienced my unique talent for creating more chaos than productivity, he decided it was time to pass me on to someone else. Apparently, he thought I'd "done enough" for his business, and, in a stroke of inspiration, he convinced my Uncle Wolfy to take me under his wing. Now, Morris and Uncle Wolfy were practically brothers themselves, so it was like I was being "handed down" in the family. The only catch? Wolfy wasn't exactly thrilled with the idea. Let's just say he wasn't jumping up and down to pass on his welding expertise to his notoriously destructive nephew. And to be honest, I was a bit scared of him back then, too—he had this stern look that said, "Don't even think about it."

I was 17, eager to prove myself, and it took us a bit to warm up to each other. But once we got past the "I hope you don't destroy my entire shop" phase, I realised just how incredible he was. He had a depth of skill and a way of teaching that stuck with me. Wolfy signed me up for college at Birome Street in Liverpool, and for five years, I threw myself into learning everything I could about welding. Cast iron, aluminium, stainless steel—you name it, I was studying it. One day a week at college and 70-plus hours a week with Wolfy, absorbing everything like a sponge.

(Did I also mention he was an amazing stage hypnotist?)

What I didn't realise at the time was that this path, this trade I'd never even considered, would end up changing my life forever. It was the beginning of a career that was both challenging and rewarding, all thanks to a brother who loved me enough to hand me off and an uncle who took a chance on a kid known more for breaking things than building them. Looking back, I can't believe how lucky I was.

Chapter 21: Jackie, who changed my life; and she had no idea how much

Things were finally looking up! I had a trade, I loved welding, and for once, life seemed to be on the right path. Then, along came Jackie—the love of my life. She would change everything.

We met at this Jewish party at the SHE Club, and, before I knew it, we were sitting on a settee, chatting like we'd known each other since birth. Hours went by in easy conversation, and I'm thinking, "This is great!" But little did I know, Jackie had a plan of her own.

By the end of the night, she'd gone and told everyone at the party that we were "going out." Going out?! I had no idea—I thought I'd just had a good chat. Meanwhile, she's got us practically picking out wedding colours. I was 17! One day I'm a single welder, the next day I'm in a relationship I didn't even know I was in!

Fast forward six months. We're talking, laughing, and I, in a moment of total stupidity, say, "Wouldn't it be funny if we got engaged?" Now, to me, this was obviously a joke. But not to Jackie. Nope, she hears the word "engaged" and skips right to "we're getting married!" Next thing I know, everyone's congratulating us on our engagement, and I'm just standing there thinking, Bloody hell, what just happened? My brain's still trying to catch up while she's out buying engagement rings!

And then comes the big one: meet the parents. Now, if you've seen Meet the Parents, you'll understand. But this was worse—this was "Meet the Family." I walk in, and it's like an interrogation. Her mum's eyeing me up and down, her dad's giving me the "hurt-her-and-you're-dead" look, and the aunts and uncles are practically circling me like I'm the evening's main attraction. I've never sweated so much in my life.

Life had taken a serious detour, and the only thing in my head was, "What could possibly go wrong?"

A lot more than I expected.

Nothing ever goes smoothly, as you can probably imagine, and things were about to change drastically. Just when I thought I had a handle on the whole "surprise engagement" and "meet the family" situation, life decided to toss in a few more curveballs. It's like the universe took one look at me and thought, "Oh, he thinks he's got this? Let's spice things up."

From that moment on, it was a rollercoaster. The kind where you're holding on for dear life, screaming, "How did I even get here?" And let's just say, the adventure was only beginning.

What I haven't told you is that my dad wasn't Jewish by birth. But in every way that mattered, he was as Jewish as anyone could be. He raised me to be proud of who I am, and he embraced our faith and our culture like it was his own. According to tradition, if your mother's Jewish, then so are you—so I was raised Orthodox, with all the beliefs and customs that came with it. But this was part of who I was, of who we were, and my father was central to that.

When Jackie's mother, Alma, found out that my father wasn't Jewish by birth, she wasn't pleased. In fact, she decided she didn't want him at our wedding. To her, it was a question of tradition, of keeping the peace with her more religious family, particularly her aunt.

But to me? This was my father we were talking about. There was no way on this earth he wasn't going to be there. This wasn't a compromise I could make. My father had been my strength through every challenge, and there was no way I'd let him be excluded on the most important day of my life.

It felt like I was caught in a crossfire. Alma was adamant—determined not to upset her family's expectations, but at the cost of hurting her own daughter and, honestly, jeopardising our future together. Meanwhile, my own family didn't make it easy either. After my mum passed, she'd been the glue holding everything together, and without her, they'd grown more distant from my dad. Some of them didn't want him at the wedding either, and I remember the day I was pulled aside, brought into an office, and told that he wasn't a good father, that he'd moved on too quickly and forgotten me. They fired every insult they could at him, hoping I'd give in.

But that was never going to happen. My dad was more than family; he was my best friend, even though circumstances had left me living with my auntie. In hindsight, that move to my auntie's was one of the best things that ever happened to me. It gave me strength and resilience. But through everything, my loyalty to my father never wavered. And in that moment, I knew; no matter the pressure or what anyone said, I wouldn't let go of the people I loved. Not then, not ever.

It wasn't easy, but standing up for him was the right thing to do, and it became a defining moment in my life.

Before all the challenges, the struggles, and everything that was about to come, there was this one perfect memory—a time when it was just me and Jackie, and nothing else mattered. We needed an engagement ring, and even though I was only earning £10 a week, I saved every bit of it. I was determined to get her something beautiful. Looking back, that moment feels like a precious gem, a memory that shimmers with colour and meaning, like a rainbow of emotions I can still feel.

I remember every detail: Jackie was wearing a grey duffle coat, a woolly hat, and a scarf, her cheeks flushed from the cold, but to me, she was just... breath-taking. She looked so beautiful, so completely herself. Tears come to my eyes even now as I recall that moment. I felt like I was standing next to someone magical, someone who lit up my world just by being there.

We went to Robinson's, the jeweller's, and it felt like a dream, picking out a ring together. She chose a stunning diamond cluster—simple, elegant, perfect, just like her. As she slipped it onto her finger, I felt a sense of awe, like I was making the most important promise of my life. That ring symbolised everything I wanted with her—a lifetime, a future, a love that could withstand anything.

Even now, that memory remains one of the brightest in my heart. A moment of pure love, untouched by the world around us. It was a gift, and I'll carry it with me forever.

The pressure on us, especially on me, became unbearable. The arguments started—small things at first, but with all the strain, they grew. I knew, deep down, that if this continued, we'd both end up heartbroken. So, I made the hardest decision of my life. I broke the engagement. Jackie was distraught, and every part of me wanted to stay, to comfort her. But I knew that if I let us go down that path, the weight of everything around us would eventually tear us apart.

I walked away, carrying the ache of that choice. I knew it was for the best, but the pain of leaving her like that was something I never expected. I still feel it sometimes, the weight of that moment, knowing that sometimes love means letting go—even when it breaks your heart.

Months went by, but my feelings for Jackie didn't fade. They only grew stronger, pulling me back to her like a magnet. Eventually, we found our way back to each other, hoping—desperately—that maybe things would be different this time. Maybe her mum would change her mind, see how much we cared for each other. And for a little while, it felt like everything was finally falling into place. I could see a future, one where we'd be together despite everything. What could possibly go wrong?

Turns out, everything.

The same roadblocks, the same resistance from her mum—nothing had changed. And slowly, it wore us down. The arguments started again, fuelled by a frustration neither of us could shake. Her mum didn't seem to realise the damage she was causing, how much it hurt both of us, how it threatened to pull us apart.

Eventually, we broke up again, feeling torn between the love we had for each other and the relentless pressure that made us feel like we couldn't be together. It was one of the hardest decisions I've ever faced—walking away, knowing I still loved her, but feeling trapped in a cycle we couldn't escape. Sometimes love isn't enough to overcome everything, and realising that hurt more than I could have imagined.

I felt like a yo-yo, constantly swinging back and forth between hope and heartache with Jackie. What I didn't mention is that she was an actress; she'd even been in the last series of The Liver Birds. I used to see her on TV and feel this incredible mix of pride and longing—it was like she was somehow always close, yet out of reach. No matter how hard I tried, I couldn't shake the feeling that we were meant to be together. And just as quickly as we'd drifted apart, we'd find ourselves back together again.

This time, things felt different. Mandy, Jackie's niece, and her husband, Yoval, had moved in with Alma. Yoval had come from Israel to start a new life in England, and he and I became the best of friends. We shared dreams, struggles, and the same determination to build something meaningful here. I felt like things were finally finding their balance.

But then, everything shifted. Alma and Mandy had a huge argument one day. In a moment of heated anger, Alma told Mandy and Yoval to leave, to go out in the street with nowhere to go. She was incredibly loving in so many ways, but she could also be stubborn to a fault. Despite her warmth, her temper had a way of flaring that sometimes hurt the very people she cared about most.

I couldn't let them face that kind of uncertainty. They were family now, and you don't just turn your back on family. So I went to my uncle Wolfy and explained everything. Without a moment's hesitation, he stepped up. He offered Yoval a job, and together, we found them an apartment to help them get back on their feet.

Those days, filled with love, loyalty, and even the challenges we faced, made me realise what it truly means to stand by the people you care about. It's one of the most powerful things we can do—being there, even in the hardest moments, to lift each other up.

I was still with Jackie, but the arguments were wearing me down. I couldn't shake the resentment over what Alma had done, and the uncertainty of our future together was a weight I couldn't ignore. Finally, I decided it was over—really over this time. I figured it was time to let my family know, so I used a bit of "strategic storytelling," letting them believe it was mostly because of what happened with Yoval. But, if I'm being honest, deep down, a big part of it was about my dad and all the complications that had come with that.

Of course, things never go that smoothly, right? Weeks go by, and I end up with a nasty cold—the kind that feels like you're knocking on death's door. I'm sweating through the sheets, shivering under blankets, when there's this knock at the door. Jackie's outside, screaming and crying, desperate to see me. I could feel my heart breaking, so I buried my head under the pillow, thinking "If I see her now, we'll end up right back where we started." Eventually, she left, and I thought maybe—just maybe—I could finally move on.

As my flu lifted, I started reading Exodus, a novel about Israel. Inspired, I made a decision that surprised even me—I was going to visit Yoval and Mandy in Israel. They'd moved back and were living on a kibbutz in Afikim. My cousin Graham decided to join me, so we planned a trip for a few months. I was finally feeling a sense of direction and relief, thinking I'd get away, gain some clarity. But, just as I'm getting over the flu, guess who knocks on the door again?

Yep, Jackie's mum. Alma herself. And this time? She's telling me they want me back, saying my dad can sit at the top table at the wedding—everything I'd fought for, laid out on a silver platter. It was like she'd prepared a full sales pitch, right down to promising me the one thing I'd thought impossible.

But there I was, feeling like the world's worst negotiator, finally being offered everything I'd wanted—and it was too late. Somehow, what I'd been holding onto had already slipped through my fingers.

You're absolutely right—I couldn't get Jackie out of my mind. So I arranged to meet her, and from the moment we saw each other, it was like no time had passed. The feelings were all still there, for both of us. I told her I was heading to Israel for a bit, but maybe when I got back, we could meet up again? She gave me this big smile and said, "Of course." I felt like a teenager all over again.

It was May when we finally touched down in Israel, and before I knew it, I was at the kibbutz with Yoval. He was thrilled and started hinting I should live there full-time. And let me tell you, it was amazing—the sun, the people, the food, everything. But there was one slight hiccup: all I could think about was Jackie. Even while living this incredible adventure, my heart was back in England with her. That's when I knew—there was no escaping it. I couldn't live without her.

So, in true romantic style, I started sending letters. Love letters, would you believe it? Here I was, pouring my heart out on paper, feeling like some character from a classic film. When I finally got back to the UK, I felt on top of the world. Jackie and I met up, and it was like we'd never been apart. Everything just fell right back into place.

Life was feeling perfect. It really felt like nothing could go wrong now, like we'd conquered every obstacle. But... you guessed it. What could possibly go wrong?

Well, you're about to find out.

Chapter 22: This was the moment when everything changed

My life was on the brink of a massive shift, and I could feel it. The decisions I was about to make weren't just about today—they were about every day to come. They would shape my entire future, and there was no going back. I stood there, realising that from here on, every step, every choice, would determine the course of my life. This was the moment when everything changed.

Now it was time to meet the family—again. This time, Alma decided to bring backup, showing up with her husband, Leon. My family could hardly believe it! We were all wondering if this time, things might actually go smoothly... but, knowing our luck, we were probably in for a few surprises. Buckle up—meeting the family was about to take on a whole new level of excitement!

They went alone to meet my family, and Jackie and I stayed back, hoping that maybe, just maybe, things would finally settle. The wedding was on, and I kept telling myself nothing could stop it now. But when Alma and Leon came back, I could sense something was wrong. To this day, I don't know exactly what was said, but I've pieced together that Alma might've asked my family to buy a house for Jackie and me. Looking back, it feels like a naive hope; they weren't even close to seeing me as their son, so why would they support my future with her?

Then came the hardest blow. The next day, back at my auntie's, my uncle called me into his office. He looked at me with a seriousness I'll never forget and told me, point-blank, to cancel the wedding. He said, "None of us will be there." At that moment, it hit me like a punch to the chest. They wanted me to give up the person I loved, to cancel the life Jackie and I had been dreaming of together. It hurt beyond words.

I was left feeling like I'd been standing on solid ground that suddenly crumbled beneath me. They had no right to ask me to end my own wedding, and in that instant, I realised how alone I truly was in this decision. But I also knew I had to hold on to Jackie, no matter the cost.

I genuinely believed they'd come around. With the wedding booked and everything moving forward, I kept thinking that as the days drew closer, my family would find it in their hearts to soften, to remember the love we'd once shared. But with every passing day, it was as if I became invisible to them. My aunt, my uncle, even my cousin—who'd been like a brother—turned their backs on me. They'd sent me to Coventry, a silent rejection that cut through me like a knife. The thought of my mum... she would have been devastated. I could almost feel her spirit beside me, watching the family she'd held so close now push me so far away.

Every night, after I'd been with Jackie, I'd come home close to midnight, hoping that somehow things had changed, that they'd left the door unlocked for me. But time after time, the door was bolted shut. So I slept in the car, feeling the chill of the night settle in, letting it seep into my bones and heart. At dawn, they'd unlock the door without a word, and I'd step inside, pull on my overalls, and get ready for work. My uncle, who lived just a few doors down, would pull up in his blue transit van with my aunt beside him, and we'd drive in a heavy silence that filled every inch of that van. Not a word, not a look—just this unbearable wall of rejection and judgement surrounding me.

Every day, I ached from it, but I refused to give in. I knew that Jackie and I were meant to be together, and nothing they could do would change that. But night after night, I'd come back to that locked door, the rejection slamming down on me harder each time. I started calling my best friend, who didn't even hesitate to offer me his spare room, saying, "Come stay whenever you need." It was a relief to feel even a shred of kindness and support.

Looking back on it now, writing this, the memories bring that ache right back to the surface. I feel the tears as I remember that deep loneliness, the sting of being so completely abandoned by those I loved most. I didn't realise how heavy it would be, how much it would still affect me after all this time. I wanted so much for them to stand by me, but I was left standing alone.

Just when I thought things couldn't possibly get any worse, they did. You'd think there was only so much one person could go through, but life had more in store. I had convinced myself—really believed—that my family would eventually come around, that they would realise this was my happiness and somehow, they'd accept it. But I was wrong. So wrong.

Every day, they treated me as if I didn't exist, like I was already dead to them. It was a haunting feeling—to be living under the same roof as people I once loved, people who had once been my world, only to be met with silence and cold glances. The only warmth in my life was at Jackie's. Alma, her mother, had come to feel like my own, and with them, I finally felt like I belonged.

Then I'd come home, late as usual, and there it was—the locked door. I can still feel that ache; that sinking sadness and gnawing fear as I stood in the cold, shut out from my own family. When the door finally unlocked in the morning, I'd slip inside, and though I was back in the house, I knew in every way that mattered I was still very much outside.

I was working 75 hours a week for next to nothing, trying to keep going, holding onto Jackie and the future we wanted. But one day, I was called into the office. My uncle sat there with a stack of letters—applications I'd sent to oil companies long before any of this happened, back when I still thought about building a future for myself. Letters that, in my mind, were a sign of ambition, of hope.

But to them? They were something else entirely. They didn't see a young man looking for a future; they saw someone trying to escape them, and they didn't like it. It was as though they thought they owned me, like I had no right to dream beyond their reach.

Then came the final blow. My uncle looked at me, cold and resolute, and told me to cancel the wedding. When I refused, he fired me on the spot. Just like that—years of loyalty, all those hours, gone.

He looked me in the eye and said, "You're sacked." I was stunned. My chest felt heavy, and before I could stop myself, the tears just came. I walked out of that office with my heart shattered, drove back to my auntie's, packed my suitcase, and left.

As I closed that door behind me, there was a sadness so deep I didn't know if I'd ever come back from it. But beneath it, there was also a hint of relief, maybe even strength—a feeling that somehow, despite everything, I'd finally reclaimed a piece of myself.

But, of course, life wasn't finished with me yet. The journey was far from over.

As the wedding drew closer, I decided I needed to face them—all of them. I went to see my brother Morris and his wife first, practically begging them to come, to set aside whatever it was that held them back. They looked at me, and I'll never forget the finality in their voices as they said, "United we stand." I went to each and every one of them—the family I'd grown up with, the ones in Liverpool who'd seen me through my childhood, my hardest moments. I hoped for even a glimmer of understanding, but all I met was resistance, as if a wall had been built around them. One by one, they refused.

We sent invitations to everyone, hoping that maybe something would shift. But when they came back, ripped to shreds, my heart sank. It was a rejection deeper than words, as if they were trying to erase the very idea of my wedding, my happiness. It hurt in a way I can hardly describe, knowing that I'd done nothing but follow my heart that my only "mistake" was wanting a life with Jackie.

And yet, even now, after all these years, I feel no resentment toward them. I can't. They are my family, the people who shaped me, and to this day, I won't allow anyone to speak poorly of them. They made me who I am, gave me strength, resilience, and a heart that still loves fiercely despite everything.

But, I'd be lying if I said it didn't leave scars. When the wedding day came and went, and they didn't come, it felt like a piece of me had been left behind. Twenty years passed before I spoke to any of them again. It's a wound that time has softened but never truly healed.

But there was more to face, another hurdle I hadn't anticipated. In the Jewish tradition, I needed someone to stand with me, someone who was Jewish and had married within the faith.

Bentley, my brother, was the one I hoped would be there for me. He was truly the only one in my life, someone I could trust. But, just like the rest of the family, he couldn't fulfil that role—he'd married outside the faith. So I thought of my Aunt May, the one person I believed might set all the disagreements aside and stand with me.

It was a beautiful summer's day, close to the wedding, and I felt a flicker of hope as I called her. I explained what I needed, and for a moment, I held my breath, hoping she'd hear what this meant to me. But her response was the same: "United we stand."

Just like that, any last thread I'd been holding on to fell away. My family had truly turned their backs, and now, on one of the most important days of my life, I'd have to find someone else to stand by my side.

In the end, I had to ask someone I'd never even met—a relative of Jackie's mum—to walk me down the aisle. It wasn't how I'd imagined it. My heart ached with the realisation that the people who'd raised me, the ones I'd thought would always be there, weren't just absent—they'd closed the door on this part of my life completely.

The day of the wedding arrived—June 26th. It was a beautiful day, the kind of day where you can feel the world is full of promise. My dad, my brother, and my best friend were there with me, their presence bringing strength and comfort in a way words can't capture.

But still, a part of me held onto a fragile hope, a quiet wish that somehow, against all odds, the rest of my family might change their minds and show up. I watched the doors, my heart flickering with each moment that passed, but deep down, I knew—they wouldn't be there.

And then it struck me: I didn't need their permission to find happiness. My path was my own, and it didn't matter who approved or disapproved.

I was here, standing beside the love of my life, ready to step into a future that was filled with so much promise and joy. In that moment, I knew my life was going to be magical, no matter who chose to stand beside me.

Chapter 23: Sadness that stays with you for a lifetime

And so, the journey of life begins—a path filled with unknowns, twists, and turns, but also with endless possibilities and moments of joy. It's a journey where love and resilience become our compass, where each step forward is a step into a future shaped by hope and courage.

No matter who is beside us or who we have to leave behind, this journey is ours to walk, and every moment ahead is waiting to be lived fully. Here's to embracing it, with open hearts and unwavering strength.

When you look back, really look back, it's like peeling back layers you thought had long since healed. The memories resurface, raw and vivid, and suddenly, the pain you tried so hard to block out comes rushing in as if it never left. It's as though those old hurts were just waiting, quietly tucked away, until the moment you allowed yourself to remember.

You begin to feel each one, reliving the past, and for a moment, it's as if no time has passed at all. Those wounds, once buried, remind you of the strength it took to move forward—of all the parts of yourself you had to rebuild along the way.

When I look back at my life—the moment my dad sent me to live with my auntie, my brother stepping in and arranging for my uncle to teach me a trade, meeting Jackie and falling in love, the beautiful chaos of marriage, and raising five incredible children—it all feels like pieces of a puzzle that somehow fell perfectly into place.

None of it seems random; every twist and turn, even the hardest parts, feel like they were meant to lead me right here.

It makes me wonder—was it the universe quietly orchestrating this path for me, or could it be that, somehow, we set our own lives into motion long before we were even born?

Chapter 24: The Great Bunk Bed Incident: How I Almost Turned a School Trip into a Crime Scene

I have to tell you this story—it's one of those moments you'll laugh at later but want to crawl into a hole about at the time. It all started when I was 13, on a school trip to Israel. You know those trips where everyone is meant to bond and make memories? Well, I made a memory, all right—a legendary disaster.

We were staying in this dorm with bunk beds and those massive metal lockers that look like they were designed to survive an apocalypse. I'm up on the top bunk, minding my own business, reading, when along comes Simon. Now, Simon was that one kid who seemed to think annoying people was a full-time job.

He starts poking me, laughing, being a general pain. "Simon, stop it," I say, trying to stay calm. But does Simon stop? No. Why would he? If anything, my frustration only fuelled him. "Simon, STOP IT!" I snapped, hoping that'll do it. It didn't. Simon hears "stop" and translates it to "go harder."

And that's when I made my fatal mistake. Without thinking, I raise my foot and shove him—just enough to get him to back off. Or so I thought. Instead of a harmless stumble, Simon goes flying. And I mean flying. He sails off the bed in a way that would impress an Olympic diver, and lands with a horrifying THUNK right into the sharp point of the metal locker, which entered the side of his head. Everything goes silent. Simon doesn't move. My heart stops. In that moment, I'm certain I've killed him. This is it. Goodbye school, hello life in prison. Then, finally, he stirs. Relief! But then I see his head—swelling up like a balloon on fast-forward. My panic levels go through the roof.

The teacher rushes in, demanding to know what happened. I'm ready to confess to murder when Simon—bless his annoying little soul—says nothing. Not a word. They whisk him off to the hospital, and I'm left pacing the dorm, imagining the headlines: "13-Year-Old Turns School Trip into Crime Scene."

Hours later, Simon returns, head wrapped in bandages like a Halloween costume gone wrong. The teacher gives us the grim news: the injury was millimetres away from his temple. Any closer, and it could've been catastrophic. My stomach flips. Meanwhile, Simon? Oh, he's living his best life, playing the role of the injured hero.

And then the real torture begins. Simon uses his silence as leverage. For the next two weeks, I'm his personal assistant. "Get me water. Carry my bag. Do my chores." I'm practically bowing every time he enters the room. But honestly, I'm so grateful he didn't rat me out, I just go with it.

Looking back now, it's hilarious—kind of. But it's also a stark reminder: never underestimate how quickly a tiny shove can turn into an international incident. And never mess with Simon. The kid might be indestructible, but my nerves are not.

As time went on, two remarkable things happened. First, Simon, the same kid I once sent flying off a bunk bed in a fit of frustration, went on to become an English physiologist, biochemist, and a pioneering specialist in in-vitro fertilisation (IVF). It's surreal to think that the boy I thought I'd seriously injured that day grew into someone whose work has brought life and hope to so many families.

It's a humbling reminder of how life unfolds in unexpected ways—how moments we look back on with guilt or regret can be part of a story much bigger than ourselves. Simon's journey from that dormitory to changing the world through science is a testament to resilience, growth, and the surprising paths our lives can take. Looking back now, I feel both pride and gratitude for having been a small, albeit chaotic, chapter in his incredible story.

Well, it doesn't end there—because life has a way of tying things together in the most unbelievable ways. Turns out, Simon Fishel, the same Simon who became a world-renowned physiologist, biochemist, and IVF pioneer, is actually Jackie's first cousin. How incredible is that?

It's almost too wild to believe. The boy I nearly sent to the ER during that chaotic school trip is not just a remarkable scientist but also directly connected to someone in my life. It feels like the universe weaving an intricate tapestry, connecting people and moments in ways you'd never expect. It's a small world, isn't it? Or maybe it's just life's funny way of reminding us how interconnected we all are.

Chapter 25: The Amazing (and Often Ridiculous) Journey of My Life

Life, as I've lived it, has been nothing short of an unpredictable rollercoaster—filled with love, loss, laughter, and moments so absurd that they belong in a sitcom. Yes, there were heartbreaks, challenges that tested me to my core, but there were also moments so hilariously chaotic that I often found myself wondering, "Is this really happening?" Let me take you on a whirlwind tour of this amazing, messy, ridiculous journey that I've been on.

If there's one thing I've learned, it's that parenting is less about having all the answers and more about being really good at pretending you do. Imagine juggling five kids, a rebellious teenager, and the occasional existential crisis. Now add a turkey running loose in the house (yes, that happened), and you've got a snapshot of my life.

One time, I tried to have a "serious family meeting," only to have one of the kids interrupt by asking, "Why do you have a sock stuck to your back?" Dignity? Out the window. But laughter? That was always in good supply.

Through it all—the chaos, the tears, the smashed vases, and the runaway turkeys—one thing has been constant: laughter. It's what kept me grounded when everything else felt overwhelming. It's what bound our family together, even in the darkest times. And it's what turns even the hardest memories into stories worth telling.

So, if you're reading this, I hope you laugh. I hope you see the joy hidden in life's absurdities. Because if there's one thing my journey has taught me, it's this: you can't always control what happens, but you can always find a reason to smile—especially when you're chasing a mouse around the kitchen.

Chapter 26: The Munchkin Men Strike Again: Shanna's Birthday Surprise Gone Wrong!

Alright, get ready for this one—it's a classic. Picture the scene: it's Shanna's 15th birthday, and the twins, Joshua and Zak, have just turned 3. Shanna's having the time of her life, all her friends are over, the house is packed, everyone's brought gifts—it's like a small toy store exploded on her bed. We've got all sorts of presents piled up, waiting for her to open them after the party. What could possibly go wrong? (Yes, I should know better by now.)

The party's amazing, Shanna's thrilled, and the last friend finally leaves. Shanna can barely contain herself, racing up the stairs to her room to open her presents. But then we hear this almighty scream. Jackie and I dash upstairs, wondering what on earth has happened, and there it is—the scene of utter destruction.

There, right in the middle of Shanna's room, are Joshua and Zak, faces covered in chocolate, looking like two mini burglars who got caught mid-heist. Every present has been unwrapped; they didn't just open the chocolate ones—they opened everything. They've got lipstick smeared all over the walls, the bed, their faces... They basically turned the room into a Jackson Pollock masterpiece of chaos.

I can't help it—I burst out laughing. Jackie's trying to keep a straight face, which is impossible when she turns to them and says, "You two are officially the Munchkin Men." They look up, totally oblivious, like this is all just a normal Tuesday for them. Meanwhile, poor Shanna's standing there, staring at her half-eaten, smudged presents like her world has just crumbled.

Honestly, do you think it's inherited? Because at this point, the family talent for chaos seems to be genetic.

Chapter 27: Dinner Disaster: The Day I Became the Main Course

It was just one of those days—you know, the kind where the universe seems to have a personal vendetta. I'm with Jackie, off to meet friends for a meal at the Albert Docks in Liverpool. The vibe is perfect: good company, great setting, and plenty of laughs. What could possibly go wrong? Oh, just everything.

So there we are, chatting away, and I decide to stand up—simple, right? Wrong. Out of nowhere, I walk smack into a waiter carrying what I can only describe as the most over-ambitious tray of food in restaurant history.

Suddenly, it's like slow motion. The waiter goes one way, I go the other, and the tray? Well, the tray does a majestic pirouette in the air, scattering food and drinks like some bizarre Michelin-starred fireworks display.

Before I even know what's hit me—well, besides the tray—I'm on the floor, absolutely covered in glass, gravy, and what I can only hope is mashed potato. The waiter was sprawled out in the opposite direction, looking like they'd just been taken out by a WWE wrestler.

Meanwhile, the entire restaurant has gone deadly silent, every pair of eyes locked on me like I'm the halftime entertainment.

Jackie and my friends? Oh, they're laughing so hard they can barely breathe. Me? I'm just lying there thinking, "This cannot be my life?" Honestly, if they'd handed me a mop and apron right then, I'd have started cleaning up out of pure shame.

Of course, apologies all around—no problem, accidents happen, right? So, we finished the meal. Well, they did. I was too busy picking bits of food out of my hair, like I'd suddenly decided to model the "plated dinner" look. A stray chip here, a splash of gravy there—it was a culinary crime scene, and I was the victim.

Eventually, we head home, me trying to laugh it off but secretly dreading the damage. Then comes the next morning. I wake up, stroll to the mirror, and—oh no. I look like I've gone ten rounds with Mike Tyson. Both eyes, black as coal. Trust me, it wasn't the food. Unless they were secretly serving heavyweight punches as a side dish.

At that point, all I could do was laugh. I mean, what else can you do when your face tells the story of the most chaotic dinner in Albert Docks history?

Chapter 28: The Yellow Mini Bomb Scare: Who Needs Enemies with Advice Like This?

Alright, where do I even begin with this one? I'm about 25, and back then, being Jewish came with some "special" concerns. Letter bombs, car bombs—basically, if it could go "boom," it was on our radar. So here I am, driving a bright yellow Mini—you know, just in case anyone missed me—and living with Jackie in an apartment block with its own little car park.

One morning, I go outside, and there's my Mini, parked smack dab in the middle of the car park, like it's trying to get attention. Now, I know I didn't leave it there. I go back up to the apartment, tell Jackie, and she just gives me this look like, "Oh, brilliant, what now?"

So I think, "Right, better call the police—this could be serious." I get on the line, explain the situation, mention that I'm Jewish, and with all the recent car bomb threats, I'm worried someone might have put one in my tiny yellow spotlight of a car. And do you know what the genius on the other end says?

"Well, why don't you drive it over, and we'll check it for you."

Excuse me?! I'm sitting there, phone in hand, jaw on the floor, thinking, Drive it over? Like, literally drive a potential bomb through traffic? "Sure thing, officer! Let me just pop a 'Wide Load' sign on the back and pray I don't take half the city with me if I hit a speed bump."

Honestly, with advice like that, who even needs a security threat?

Chapter 29: The chandelier explodes into a million tiny pieces, raining down

I have to tell you something upfront—I am totally accident-prone. Seriously. You wouldn't believe the things that have happened to me, but trust me, these are all true stories. One particular incident stands out, back when I was 17 and had just passed my driving test. To earn a bit of extra cash, I used to help my brother with his upholstery and French polishing business. This was back in the days before IKEA or MFI, so people actually got their furniture polished, can you imagine?

Anyway, one Saturday, my brother asked me and two other guys to pick up a three-piece suite, a double wardrobe, a chest of drawers, and a dressing table that all needed to be polished. Simple enough, right? Well, we didn't have fancy GPS or sat-nav back then—just a trusty A-to-Z map. And, of course, it didn't help that this place wasn't even on the map.

Hours and hours of driving later, we finally found it. We're in the middle of the Welsh countryside, deep in the outback, and there's this tiny terraced house—one of five, and so far out, it felt like we were picking up furniture from a fairy tale. I knocked on the door, and this lady answered. She immediately looked concerned, probably because the three of us didn't exactly scream "professional." One guy was about 22 stone, the other was skinny as a rake, and then there was me—still a kid at the time.

The lady says, "You will be careful, won't you? We've just had the house painted, the plastering's been done, walls knocked down, and it was only finished yesterday."

Being the confident (read "clueless") 17-year-old I was, I assured her, "Don't worry, Mrs. Jones, we're professionals. There's nothing to worry about!" And funny enough, her name actually was Mrs. Jones. That should've been my first warning sign.

Now, picture this: we're carrying furniture down the world's narrowest staircase, with a beautiful chandelier hanging dead-centre, just waiting for disaster. We made our way upstairs to the bedroom and started dismantling the furniture to pack it safely into the van—starting with the chest of drawers. First, we took out all the drawers, no problem. Next came the base.

And that's where things took a turn. Let's just say, you'll want to keep reading to find out what happened next. Mrs. Jones was not as calm as I was about to be.

Next up: the wardrobe. And when I say wardrobe, I mean this thing was the size of a small country. It weighed a ton, and I'm pretty sure the house was constructed around it. No way to take it apart, so we had to move it as-is, because why not?

And this is where everything went to hell.

Alright, picture this: me—Mr. 22-stone, sweating buckets just from thinking about the staircase—and Skinny McGee, who probably weighs less than the wardrobe we're trying to wrestle, attempting to navigate this monster down a staircase about as wide as a pencil. If you've ever seen that episode of Friends where they're trying to get the couch up the stairs—"Pivot! Pivot!"—yeah, this was worse. Way worse.

We get halfway down, and—surprise!—the wardrobe gets completely jammed between the walls. Stuck. Like, really, truly stuck. Now, I'm hanging off the thing like some kind of wannabe Tarzan, trying to yank it free. But all I'm achieving is ripping off chunks of plaster that just yesterday had been freshly done. Beautiful, smooth plaster... now crumbling like a biscuit.

Just then, Mrs. Jones pops her head around the corner with a smile that could light up the room and says, "Would you boys like a cup of coffee?" COFFEE! I'm dangling off her wardrobe like a circus act, and this woman is offering caffeine like we're having a polite tea party. Of course, she can't see the disaster unfolding behind the wardrobe. I managed to croak out, "No, thank you!" through clenched teeth as she happily skips back into the kitchen, blissfully unaware her house is slowly being demolished.

After what felt like hours of swinging from this wardrobe like I'm auditioning for Cirque du Soleil, I finally yanked it free—and straight into the ceiling. And guess what was hanging from that ceiling? Yep, a chandelier. Not just any chandelier, but one that I'm pretty sure came straight out of Buckingham Palace.

Smash! The chandelier explodes into a million tiny pieces, raining down on us like glitter at a disco from hell. Now, there's a gaping hole in the ceiling, and the beautiful plaster? Well, let's just say it's now a distant memory.

We didn't stick around to admire our handiwork. Nope, we shoved that wardrobe into the van faster than you could say, "Let's get out of here before Mrs. Jones sees what we've done." But, of course, this is me we're talking about, so it didn't end there. Oh no. We got back, and the next thing you know, the police are involved, insurance agents are showing up, and my brother—well, let's just say he wasn't exactly giving me a high five. He had to fix all the damage for free, and Mrs. Jones got a very expensive freebie.

Honestly, looking back, it would've been cheaper to pay me to stay away. And trust me, this is just the tip of the iceberg when it comes to my accidental destruction skills. Stay tuned—there's more where this came from.

Chapter 30: Sale of the century

Years ago, I used to sell windows. Sounds simple, right? Well, buckle up because this particular sale was anything but smooth. It started off like every window salesman's dream—he said yes! Then, five minutes later, he said no. Then he waffled back and forth like we were negotiating the fate of the world. By the end of it, his final answer was a firm "no," feeling like I'd just lost a game of Who Wants to Be a Millionaire?

Fuming, I stormed out of his house. Of course, because life has a sense of humour, it wasn't just drizzling. Nope, it was full-on, apocalyptic-style rain. Buckets. I felt like I needed a canoe to get back to my car. So there I am, muttering to myself about this guy's indecision and why I didn't get the sale, while looking like a wet cat that just lost a fight with a garden hose.

I fling open the car door, plop down, and angrily jam the gear stick into what I thought was reverse, fully ready to escape this disaster. Except I didn't put it in reverse. Oh no, I slammed it into first gear. I hit the gas like I was trying to flee the scene of a crime, and BAM! I shot forward straight into the car in front of me.

Now, here's the kicker: the car I smashed into? It was the client's car. I mean, could the universe be any more on point? There I was, just sitting in my car, staring at the wrecked bumper, the rain still pounding down on me, thinking, "Well, that's one way to leave a lasting impression."

I can only imagine the look on his face when he stepped out and saw me, the window guy who couldn't sell him windows, now delivering a free car crash. Let's just say, I didn't get the sale, but I did get an unforgettable story. Classic me—breaking hearts and bumpers, one sale at a time.

Chapter 31: The Door Deal of a Lifetime

You're not going to believe this story—honestly, it sounds like something out of a sitcom. So there we were, struggling financially. No safety net, no steady salary. Self-employed, commission-only, selling windows of all things. And then the cherry on this delightful sundae? I was owed £10,000 in commission, only to be told I wasn't going to get it. Oh, and did I mention this happened right before Christmas? Merry Christmas to me!

Now, imagine the scene: I had to go home and break the news to my wife. Let me tell you, that conversation did not go well. "No money? Right before Christmas? And whose fault is that?" Trust me, you don't want to be in the room for that kind of marital bonding. It was like getting grilled on every bad decision I'd ever made. I was half-expecting her to whip out a slideshow.

So what do I do? I had to suck it up, march back to that godforsaken job, swallow my pride, and apologise. Yes, apologise to the very people who'd tried to stiff me out of ten grand. I'm there, hat in hand, giving them my best sad puppy eyes, practically begging for my job back. It was humiliating. But hey, desperate times, right?

And then came the real kicker. The job itself was the stuff of nightmares. Picture this: trudging around in the freezing cold, knocking on doors, trying to convince people to spend their hard-earned money on windows when they're just trying to figure out how to pay their heating bills. Every day felt like some cruel joke. You'd think it couldn't get worse, but oh, just wait. Because what happened next? Well, you wouldn't believe it even if I told you…

Here's what happened next—and trust me, you can't make this stuff up. What I forgot to mention earlier was that after he sacked me, he casually dropped the bombshell that my commission—somewhere between £10,000 and £12,000—was actually coming. The windows were being fitted, and I was set to get the money before Christmas. Yes, the same Christmas I'd just ruined with my "we're broke" speech to my wife.

But here's the thing. The reason he sacked me wasn't just because of the usual drama—it was because I, in a moment of sheer brilliance, decided to tell him exactly what I thought of him. And not just in private—oh no, that would've been far too sensible. I called him a bloody idiot right there in front of everyone. The staff, the clients, the tea lady—whoever was in earshot got a front-row seat to my meltdown. It was less "office chat" and more "public execution of my career."

As you can imagine, that didn't go down particularly well. His face turned the kind of red you only see on fire engines, and before I knew it, I was escorted out like a troublemaker in a school assembly. At the time, I thought I was standing up for myself, speaking truth to power, being a hero. In reality? I was a bloke who'd just flushed his last bit of hope down the toilet—and six weeks before Christmas, no less.

After the argument—or should I say, after being absolutely ripped to shreds—I had to go back. Yes, I walked straight into his office, trying to muster whatever scraps of dignity I had left. I stood there, looked him square in the eye, and said, "I want my job back."

Now, his way with words? Let's just say he was quite the poet. Without missing a beat, he replied, "F*** off."

Charming, right? But I wasn't about to back down. I planted myself firmly in his office and said, "I'm not leaving here until I get my job back."

He stared at me like I'd just sprouted a second head. You see, in this business, even though you were technically "self-employed," the truth was they had you by the throat the moment you made your first sale. They controlled the commissions, the leads, the customers—basically your entire livelihood. Walking away wasn't really an option, and he knew it.

So there we were: him glowering behind his desk, and me standing there like a stubborn kid who refused to leave the sweet aisle without a lollipop. The tension was thick, but I wasn't moving. Eventually, he let out this exasperated sigh, and I could almost see the gears turning in his head. He was weighing up whether to give in or call security.

But here's the thing: I knew I had him. Because no matter how much of a sergeant major he fancied himself to be, he couldn't deny that I was good at what I did—and he wasn't about to risk losing more sales during the busiest time of year.

He looked at me, leaned back in his chair, and said with all the smugness of a man who thinks he's holding all the cards, "Alright, on one condition: it's Friday afternoon, you bring me a deal with a full deposit on my desk by 9:00 a.m. Monday morning. If not, don't bother coming back."

That was his condition. And this was mine. I knew exactly what he was like—he'd find any excuse to hold onto the money he owed me, so I pushed back. "Fine," I said, "but here's the deal: I get you a deal with a full 10% or more deposit by Monday morning, and you give me every penny you owe me. No stalling, no excuses." He stared at me for a moment, then nodded reluctantly. To his credit, he was a man of his word—eventually. When I'd actually get that money, though? Your guess was as good as mine.

With the terms set, he barked, "Go in the room and start belling. We'll give you a lead later." I didn't even hesitate. "Stick your leads," I shot back, "I'll find one myself." With that, I stormed out, got in my car, and drove home.

And then it hit me. As I sat in traffic, staring at the dashboard, the reality of the situation sank in. It was Friday night, and I had just over 48 hours to pull off a miracle. How the bloody hell am I going to get a sale with a full deposit by Monday morning?

That was the million-pound question. And trust me, what happened next was nothing short of a circus act.

Got home, walked through the door, and said, "Good news—I got my job back!" Expecting some kind of praise, I was met with the look. You know the one. My wife crossed her arms and asked suspiciously, "That wasn't so hard, was it?"

I couldn't believe what she'd just said. Not so hard? "Well," I started, "there's a small condition." She raised an eyebrow. "I have to have a deal on his desk by 9:00 a.m. Monday with a full deposit." She stared at me like I'd just announced I was running for Prime Minister.

"Oh, and if I don't," I added, quoting the boss, "'Don't bother coming back.'"

Her jaw dropped. "You've got to be kidding me."

"Good news, though!" I said, trying to sound positive. "If I do get the deal, he'll pay me all the money he owes me!"

At that, she gave me the look of doom. "Trust me," I muttered, "she wasn't happy." And honestly, looking back, I can't blame her. The whole situation was absurd. In hindsight, I should've just sent Jackie to get the deal herself. She's the one who could scare anyone into handing over a full deposit—she's got a glare that could knock the confidence out of a car salesman. But no, this was my mess, and I had to figure out how to clean it up.

Why, oh why, do I always get myself into these messes? I swear, if there's a way to make my life harder, I'll find it. It's now 4:00 p.m. on a Friday, Christmas is looming like a grumpy landlord demanding rent, and I've got exactly zero leads. The boss's words echoed in my head: "Deal on my desk by 9:00 a.m. Monday—or don't come back." No pressure, right?

So, desperate times call for desperate measures. Enter the "blowout book." Now, for the uninitiated, this is the graveyard of leads—names of people who might have wanted windows at some point in the last decade but have since disappeared into the ether. It's like trying to sell ice to someone who just bought a freezer. But hey, when you're drowning, you grab any rope you can find, even if it's frayed and covered in cobwebs.

I grabbed the book, slapped it on the table, and muttered, "Alright, you dusty old relic, let's see if you've got a Christmas miracle in you." I dove in, flipping through names with the urgency of someone defusing a bomb. Time was ticking, and the stakes couldn't have been higher—if I didn't pull this off, I'd be explaining to my wife why there'd be no presents under the tree. Again.

With all the confidence of a man who's absolutely winging it, I picked up the phone and started dialling. Each ring felt like a countdown to doom. "Come on, pick up!" I whispered on the phone like a lunatic. Finally, someone answered, and I launched into my pitch with the kind of enthusiasm only sheer desperation can fuel.

And that's where the fun really began. Let's just say not everyone was feeling the Christmas spirit—and I was about to learn just how creative people can get with their excuses.

I rang, and I rang, and I rang some more, feeling like a telemarketer with a gambling problem. By the time someone actually picked up, I was ready to propose just to keep them on the line. Then, miracle of miracles, they said the magic words: "I'm interested."

Turns out, they needed a front door. A front door! Not a full set of windows or a fancy conservatory—just one solitary door. But to me, at that moment, it was like they'd asked for Buckingham Palace. "Front door? Of course! The best decision you'll ever make!" I set the appointment for 3:00 p.m. on Sunday and hung up, clutching the phone like a trophy. This was it. My one shot.

From then on, I was laser-focused. This wasn't just a sale; it was a matter of survival. That door, priced at a hefty £780 (yes, for a door), was my lifeline. I told myself, once I got into that house, I wasn't leaving without a deal. Forget pitching a tent—I was ready to unpack sleeping bags, set up camp, and live there if necessary. I would sell that door or become part of their furniture. There was no Plan B.

That night, I couldn't sleep. I stared at the ceiling, my mind racing with scenarios. What if they changed their mind? What if they hated me? Worse, what if they were "just browsing"? The stress was real. Meanwhile, my wife, sensing my hysteria, rolled over and said, "It's a door, not brain surgery." Easy for her to say—she wasn't the one facing the Door Olympics.

By the time Sunday rolled around, I was a jittery wreck, running purely on coffee, sheer desperation, and the faint hope that I could somehow pull this off. This wasn't just about selling a door—it felt like I was fighting for my very existence. This door was the only thing standing between me and total disaster. No pressure.

Jackie, bless her, was worried. She always had my back, even when I barely believed in myself. She was the one who kept me going, the one who could somehow pull strength out of me even when I felt like I had none left. She believed in me, and that's when it hit me: I couldn't let her down. Not now. Not ever.

As I grabbed my pitch materials and headed out the door, she gave me one last look. It wasn't just a look of encouragement; it was a don't-even-think-about-coming-back-empty-handed look. And trust me, it was more motivating than anything else. With Jackie's faith in me and the weight of Christmas on my shoulders, I drove off, ready to charm the socks off anyone willing to listen. This wasn't just a door sale—this was a mission.

I arrived at the appointment, ready to give the performance of my life. Knocking on the door, I greeted Mr. Jones with the biggest smile I could muster and launched into my intro spiel like I was pitching to dragons on Dragon's Den. Of course, his wife was there too, eyeing me suspiciously at first, but they were both incredibly nice. They told me they were interested in a front door for extra security—someone had broken in three weeks earlier. I was all over it. This wasn't just a door anymore; this was their fortress.

I started my pitch, weaving in everything from durability to how this door would make their home feel like Fort Knox. Then, when I got to the price—£780—Mr. Jones practically fell out of his chair. His wife's eyebrows shot so high, I thought they were going to get stuck in her hairline.

"Look," I said, doing my best damage control, "we've got a little flexibility." Truthfully, I didn't care at this point. They were getting this door even if I had to pay for it myself. Bit by bit, I chipped away at the price, whittling it down to £450. After a bit of back-and-forth, they finally agreed. Victory was so close, I could taste it.

And then came the bombshell. "There's just one problem," Mr. Jones said. "I might be made redundant... but I won't know until January."

BLOODY JANUARY?! I need this sale now! Not in January. January wasn't going to save my Christmas, or my job, or my wife's sanity. But I stayed calm on the outside, while my brain was doing laps of pure panic on the inside.

Originally, they were planning to pay cash, but this wasn't going to work. So, I leaned in and convinced them to go with finance instead. Also there was a redundancy clause, so if he lost his job the payments would be made I reasoned, "If you are made redundant, the payments will be manageable, and you'll still have the security of the door." It took some smooth talking, but eventually, they agreed. Lowest rate possible, £50 deposit in my hand, and signatures on the dotted line.

When I walked out of that house, I didn't just feel like I'd won a sale—I felt like I'd won the lottery, the World Cup, and a lifetime supply of chocolate all at once. I strutted to my car like I'd just conquered the world, clutching that deposit like it was a golden ticket.

I drove home grinning like a Cheshire cat, practically floating on cloud nine. I couldn't wait to burst through the door and tell Jackie the good news. I'd done it. I'd bloody done it! The sale was in the bag, the deal was signed, and—best of all—it couldn't be cancelled. Yep, back then, the law was on my side. Once the ink hit the paper, it was a done deal. No buyer's remorse, no backing out.

I strutted into the house like I'd just won the Nobel Prize in Door Sales. "Jackie!" I called, practically glowing. "You're not going to believe it—I did it! I got the sale!" She looked up, a mix of relief and "about time" on her face, but I could tell she was proud.

"And you know what?" I added, puffing out my chest. "They can't cancel. It's locked in!" I might have been a little too smug, but hey, after the week I'd had, I felt like I deserved a bit of a victory lap. Jackie just smiled, shook her head, and said, "Good. Now let's hope they don't find a way to cancel."

But for me? That moment was pure magic. I'd done what felt impossible, and for the first time in days, I could actually breathe. The sale was done, Christmas was back on, and I felt like a hero—even if just for a little while.

So here we go—Monday morning, 8:30 sharp, I walk into his office like a man on a mission. I slammed the deal down on his desk, and the look on his face was priceless. He went as white as a sheet, staring at the paperwork like I'd just handed him a winning lottery ticket with his ex-wife's name on it. "Where's my money?" I asked, beaming with the confidence of someone who'd finally caught a break.

Of course, he wasn't about to make it that easy. Oh no. This was him we're talking about. He leaned back, gave me that smug, "I'm-still-in-control" grin, and said, "You'll get your money... when I'm ready."

When he's ready?! I nearly burst out laughing, except I was too busy trying not to strangle him. He wanted to keep me under his thumb, like some kind of lead-chasing puppet. But trust me; that was never going to happen.

"You'll have your money," he said, like he was doing me a favour. "Now, go in the other room, start belling, and later on, we'll give you some leads."

"Leads?" I shot back, "Stick your leads. I'll get them myself." And with that, I grabbed a phone, rolled up my sleeves, and dove into the mountain of appointment books they had stockpiled over the years. I mean, this place was like a hoarder's paradise for leads. Hundreds of dusty old books filled with names, numbers, and the occasional cryptic note like, "Interested but hates salespeople."

But you know what? I was good on the phone—no, great on the phone. I could charm the socks off anyone, and I wasn't afraid to work those blowout books like my life depended on it.

"Hello, Mrs. Smith? I see you were interested in windows... six years ago? Well, guess what! It's your lucky day because—" click.

No problem. On to the next one.

"Hi, Mr. Johnson! This is your friendly neighbourhood window expert, and—" click.

It was like speed dating with rejection, but I didn't care. With every call, I got sharper, smoother, and more determined. I was a one-man call centre, flipping through those dusty books like a caffeinated librarian on a mission. And let me tell you, by the time I found my groove, I was unstoppable. Leads or no leads, I was going to make this work. Because if there's one thing I know, it's this: you can't control someone who refuses to play by your rules.

I started making appointments—three on the first day alone—and let me tell you, I was on a mission. Each one felt like a tiny victory, and in my mind, every appointment was as good as sold. Why? Because once I got into someone's house, I was unstoppable. On the phone? I was amazed. In person? I was a force of nature. I wasn't just selling windows; I was selling dreams. Dreams with double glazing.

By the end of that day, I was booked up for the entire week. I was flying high, feeling like a sales god. But then, reality smacked me in the face: deposits. Bloody deposits. See, here's the thing—they weren't my strong suit. I could charm people into buying a houseful of windows, but getting them to hand over money upfront? Not so much.

And that's where the company had me. They didn't pay me until the windows were fitted. Fitted! Which meant weeks of waiting, during which they held all the cards—and my commission. That's how they controlled me. It was like being a kid at Christmas, staring at a pile of presents you weren't allowed to open until the Queen herself gave the okay.

But here's where I decided to flip the script. I realised if I started getting a 20% deposit upfront, I'd receive full commission right away. Suddenly, the game changed. No more waiting, no more dangling on their strings like some sort of sales marionette. They'd have no control over me—ever again.

So that was it. The new plan: no deposit, no deal. I was determined to fix my Achilles' heel, even if I had to smile, charm, and practically hypnotise people into parting with their money. By the end of that week, I wasn't just making appointments; I was securing deposits like my life depended on it. And honestly? It kind of did.

That week, I brought in £10,000 worth of business. Yep, I was flying high. And then, out of nowhere, they announced a competition. The best self-generated business would be rewarded with a promotion to Area Manager. Yes, Area Manager! The big leagues! Not only would I be selling, but I'd also get a commission from everyone on my team who sold anything. It was like becoming the boss of a mini sales army.

Week one: I marched into the office, chest puffed out, and asked, "Where's my money?" The answer? "It's on its way." Spoiler alert: it wasn't. Not a penny. But I was too busy smashing the phones to lose momentum. I was so good at booking appointments, they were practically spilling out of my ears.

The next week, I sold £20,000 worth of business. That's right—double the first week! Finally, I started receiving some commission from my previous sales. Not all of it, mind you—just enough to keep the wolves from the door. They'd drip-feed me £250 here and there like they were tossing me breadcrumbs.

It was all a game to them, you see. They thought they could control me, string me along, and keep me desperate enough to keep smashing targets for them. But here's the thing: they didn't know who they were dealing with. I wasn't just some puppet; I was a machine. I'd bring in appointment after appointment, sell like a man possessed, and all the while, I was plotting my escape from their grip.

They thought they could own me. What they didn't realise was that every £250 they handed over was just feeding the beast. The more they tried to control me, the harder I worked—not for them, but for me. Because I had one goal: to flip the script so they had no control over me ever again. And let's just say, I had a few tricks up my sleeve to make that happen.

By the fourth week, it was payday, and the Divisional Manager himself showed up—because, apparently, when you owe someone a small fortune, you send in reinforcements. I was called into the office, expecting the usual excuses, but lo and behold, they handed me not one but two cheques: £5,000 they'd owed me for ages and another £3,500 from previous business. That's £8,500 in my hand! I could barely believe it.

But then, before I could even enjoy the moment, the manager claps his hands together and shouts, "Right, let's go, everyone! Snowing outside? Perfect weather for knocking doors! Fresh air! Builds character!"

Build character? I just pocketed eight and a half grand—do you think I wanted to go knocking doors in a snowstorm? Of course not. I'm not a bloody idiot. But here's the thing: those checks weren't safe yet. They could still stop them, bounce them, or worse, suddenly "discover" a clerical error. So, I jumped up like the world's most enthusiastic door-knocker and said, "Let's go, lads! Good for your health, this is!"

So out we went, trudging through snow that felt like it was trying to turn my toes into ice cubes. But I had a plan. Oh, I wasn't there to sell—I was there to survive. While everyone else was enthusiastically pitching windows, I was strategically knocking on houses where I knew no one would answer. Dark porches, no cars in the driveway, curtains drawn—I was practically a snow detective.

"Knock, knock!" I'd say, giving it just enough effort to satisfy the manager's watchful eye. Then I'd stand there shivering, pretending to wait while secretly praying no one opened the door. Every so often, I'd scribble nonsense into my notebook, like I'd just discovered the window opportunity of the century.

By the end of the day, I was frozen solid, but my cheques were still intact, and I hadn't sold a single thing. Mission accomplished. Because in this game, sometimes the smartest move is knowing when not to play

Christmas Eve, and once again, I was the only one bringing in business. While everyone else was sipping hot cocoa and dreaming of turkey, I was out there selling like my life depended on it. Come payday, they handed me a cheque for £7,000—what they owed me—and another £5,000 for the business I'd brought in. Then, because this company loved a good performance, the boss gathered everyone around, held up my cheques like he was presenting an Oscar, and said, "This is what you earn when you work!"

Oh, so now I was a motivational poster? Fantastic. I stood there smiling, but inside, I was thinking, "Again? Using me to make a point? Give me my money, let me go home, and leave me out of your TED Talk!"

Finally, I left, cheques in hand. Jackie was on cloud nine. Bills paid, money in the bank, Christmas saved. But despite all that, I still felt like a slave to this company. And they made sure of it, too. "Back here, January 3rd, 9:00 a.m. sharp. No one is late!" Because heaven forbid we get one moment to enjoy the holidays.

Fast forward to January. Back in the office, the phones were ringing, the grind continued, and I got another cheque for £1,500. It felt like I was piecing together my income one painful week at a time. Then, out of nowhere, I remembered the competition. You know, the one they hyped up—the best self-generated business earns the crown of Area Manager. Apparently, so had everyone else. The suspense was real.

A few weeks had gone by, and in that time, I'd brought in over £100,000 worth of business. The office was buzzing. Who won? Who was going to be the company's golden child? Everyone was whispering, waiting, speculating.

And who do you think it was? Of course, it was me. Was I surprised? Not one bit. Did I feel victorious? Absolutely. Did I know they'd use this as an excuse to squeeze even more out of me? 100%.

The moment of truth had arrived. Everyone in the office was holding their breath, waiting to hear who had won the big competition. The boss stepped forward, paused for dramatic effect, and then announced, "The winner, Area Manager... Geoffrey Loveday! He did over £100,000 in six weeks, all self-generated business!" applause, pats on the back, and a big grin from the boss as he turned to shake my hand.

I accepted the handshake, looked him in the eye, and said, "Thank you." Then, without missing a beat, I added, "Oh, and by the way—stick your job."

The room went silent. You could've heard a pin drop. I didn't wait for a reaction. I turned on my heel and walked out, head high, feeling like a rock star who'd just dropped the mic.

Let me tell you, that moment felt amazing. They owed me nothing. Not a single penny. I was free—finally free—and there was nothing they could do about it. As I walked out the door, I could almost hear the chaos erupting behind me. I imagine the boss's face turned every shade of red as he sputtered something like, "Can you believe that? After all we did for him!"

And the rest of them? Probably whispering, "Did that really just happen?" Oh, it happened. And it felt fantastic.

For the first time in weeks, I felt free.

Of course, I'm not a complete lunatic—at least not entirely. After what happened last time with Jackie, you'd better believe I had a plan. I wasn't walking out into the unknown with nothing but a grin and some Christmas spirit. Nope, this time, I had already been approached by another company. Head-hunting, they called it. I called it divine timing.

The best part? I was in control. No more jumping through hoops or begging for cheques that were "on their way." Oh no, this time I made the rules. I laid it out crystal clear: upfront commissions, no games, and no boss breathing down my neck like a drill sergeant.

Jackie, of course, was in on the whole thing. She'd made it perfectly clear after the last fiasco that if I ever pulled a stunt like that again without a backup plan, I might not make it to see another Christmas. So, when I walked out of that office, it wasn't just for me—it was for us. And let me tell you, strutting into a new job on your own terms? That's a feeling money can't buy.

There were more times than I'd like to admit when I ended up back working with Gary from that same company. As much as he was a pain in the arse—and trust me, he was—I have to give the man credit. He actually taught me a lot about sales. It's just a shame he couldn't teach me how to avoid his nonsense.

One time, when I was an Area Manager, Gary pulled me aside and said, "I want you to sack someone." Fair enough—until he told me who. It was one of my best mates. The guy hadn't done anything wrong. Nothing. But Gary, in all his infinite wisdom, wanted to "shake things up" and put the fear of God into the sales team.

I looked at him, trying to keep my cool, and said, "I can't do that."

Gary didn't even flinch. He leaned in and said, "Sack him, or I'll sack you."

Now, this wasn't my first rodeo with Gary's antics, and I'd had enough. I looked him straight in the eye, smiled, and said, "You're absolutely right."

Then I grabbed my coat, stood up, and added, "Stick your job. For the last time."

I walked out, feeling the same rush of freedom as I had before, but this time, it was different. This time, I was walking away not just from Gary, but from the endless cycle of chaos he thrived on.

The funniest part? Simon—my mate I refused to sack—never even knew what happened. I didn't tell him because, honestly, why ruin the mystery? All he knew was that one day I was there, and the next, I wasn't. And let's just say, that's how I preferred it.

Chapter 32: The Day I Turned a Luton Van into a Convertible: A Masterclass in Chaos

This brings me to another one of those "you've got to be kidding me" moments. At the time, it wasn't funny at all—more like a full-blown disaster—but hey, that's me. Confident, thinking everything's going just fine... or so I'd like to believe. Remember when I said my brother should pay me to stay away? Yeah, well, the more I think about it, the more I realise I was 100% right.

So, it's late afternoon, a gorgeous summer's day—back when we actually had summers, mind you. I'd just dropped off the guys after a long day's work, when one of them asked if I could drop him off in town to buy a birthday present for his girlfriend. Of course, I said yes. I mean, what could possibly go wrong, right?

Everything.

I'm feeling good. Sunglasses on, radio blaring, the sun shining—it was one of those rare, "I've got my life together" moments. But, naturally, that feeling didn't last long. While waiting for him, I figured I'd park the van and take a little stroll around Liverpool's Seel Street. I spot a multi-story car park and think, "Perfect. I'll just drive right in."

Big mistake.

I'm driving a Luton van, and as soon as I pull in, I hear the loudest, most gut-wrenching screech you can imagine. Turns out the van was WAY too high for the car park, and I've wedged it between the concrete ceiling and the floor. Yep, the whole thing is stuck. So there I am, standing outside the van, looking at it like, "Well, this is new," while a queue of angry drivers is building up behind me, honking like their lives depend on it.

The worst part? The roof of the van is fibreglass, and there's now a massive hole in it, like I'd just taken it through a cheese grater. But wait, it gets better! I try to reverse out, and as I'm backing up, the roof of the van decides to collapse in on itself, like some kind of slow-motion horror scene. Half the roof is now sitting in the van with me. I swear, the universe was having a laugh at my expense.

But no, it doesn't end there. Oh no. As I'm desperately trying to reverse out of this death trap, I forget about the massive "FULL" and "EMPTY" which was attached to the ground. Well, it certainly lit up when I smashed into it—sending it into a thousand pieces all over the car park. I looked left, I looked right, and then I did the only thing I could think of—I bolted out of there faster than a getaway driver in a heist movie.

When I finally made it back, my brother took one look at the brand new van—and I mean brand new, he'd only picked it up that day—and he looked like he'd seen a ghost. There was fibreglass everywhere, the roof was basically missing, and all I could think was, "Yep, he's definitely going to kill me." To top it all off, I still had the audacity to ask for my wages. The man had to pay for all the damage, and I'm there like, "So, about my pay check..."

And that, my friends, is why my brother should have paid me to stay as far away from that van as humanly possible.

Chapter 33: Hanging On for Dear Life—and Laughing About It

There's one story I absolutely need to tell you. It's about my brother Bentley, who was moving from Cambridge Road in Southport. Now, he had this old Commer van, a fine piece of engineering—or so we liked to think. This is the story of how I nearly died again. Yes, again.

So, everything's packed up nicely, and we're loading the smaller items into the van. The van's got this sliding centre door, a real charming feature... unless you're resting on it. And, of course, who decides to lean on this door? Yep, me.

Now, my brother Bentley? Let's just say he drives like he's auditioning for Formula 1. We get to this roundabout, and he's taking it like he's chasing pole position. The van lurches, and wouldn't you know it? That bloody sliding door decides it's the perfect time to show off. It flies open, and suddenly, I go with it.

There I am, hanging on for dear life, half in the van and half out, with one arm gripping the edge of the door and my legs flailing around like I'm doing some sort of acrobatic stunt. The vehicle's still in motion, mind you, with Bentley completely unaware that his brother's about two seconds from becoming a permanent feature on the roundabout.

I'm yelling, "STOP THE VAN!" but the wind's whipping past so fast it probably sounds like, "AAAAAAHHH!" Eventually, he notices—or maybe it's the horrified faces of the other drivers pointing and shouting—and he slams the brakes. I somehow manage to haul myself back inside, shaking like a leaf, while Bentley looks over casually and says, "What's the problem?"

What's the bloody problem?! I nearly became a human hood ornament, that's the problem! Honestly, I don't know how I survived that one, but one thing's for sure—I'm never leaning on a sliding door again. Ever

Chapter 34: The Day My Flintstones Minivan Met Its Match: What Could Possibly Go Wrong?

Oh no, not again. What could possibly go wrong, right? Well, let me tell you—this is me we're talking about, so buckle up.

It was a beautiful summer's day, and I was driving my trusty old minivan. And when I say "trusty," I mean it was basically a Flintstones car. You know, the kind where you half-expect to use your feet to keep it moving. Seriously, you could actually see the road through the floor where the pedals were supposed to be! I'm pretty sure the only thing holding that van together was sheer willpower and maybe a bit of duct tape. But hey, back then, the law was a little more, well, lenient, shall we say.

So there I am, driving down Brodie Avenue, belting out some off-key tune, feeling the wind in my hair—because who needs air conditioning when you've got two broken windows? I'm in the zone, minding my own business, when suddenly something drops off the dashboard. Now, a sensible person would've pulled over. Me? Oh no. I looked down to see what it was, "What could go wrong?" Well, apparently, everything.

Literally a second later, I hit this car. And trust me, this car came out of nowhere. Like, I swear it materialised out of thin air just to ruin my day. My poor minivan? It folded up like an accordion, barely holding itself together, while the car I hit—a sturdy little Maxi—didn't have a single scratch. Not. One.

I get out of the van, all flustered, and you know how they tell you never to admit fault in an accident? Yeah, well, that wasn't me. I'm out there apologising like I've just run over someone's puppy, practically grovelling, "Oh my god, I'm so sorry, it's totally my fault!"

And then I see it. I look in the backseat of her car, and there's this little boy with his mouth covered in blood. My heart stops. Oh my god, what have I done? I'm standing there, convinced I've somehow caused a full-blown disaster, and I blurt out, "Is he okay?!"

She looks at me, cool as a cucumber, and says, "Oh, don't worry. He's just been to the dentist."

The dentist? I'm having a full-on heart attack thinking I've turned this poor kid into a zombie extra from a horror film, and it turns out, he's just had a tooth pulled. I didn't know whether to laugh, cry, or just lie down in the middle of the road and accept my fate.

To this day, I swear that car jumped out of a side road to ruin my life. And if there's one thing I've learned from that experience, it's this: never, ever ask, "What could possibly go wrong?" when you're driving a van held together by duct tape, dreams, and pure luck. Because trust me, the universe is always listening.

Chapter 35: The Time I Nearly Died Over a Free Meal (How to Be the Dumbest Person in the Restaurant)

Alright, buckle up, because this one's a doozy. It's one of those stories I'm really ashamed of, but, looking back, it's so absurd I can't help but laugh (and cringe). Let's get one thing straight: I'm that guy—the one who pretends to have his life together, confidently strutting around like I know where I'm going in life. Spoiler alert: I don't. Not even a little.

So, picture this: Jackie and I are out for dinner with friends. Sounds normal, right? Except... financially, things were a disaster. You know the type of broke where you mentally calculate how much tap water you can drink without getting charged? Yeah, that level of broke. But hey, here we are, at a fancy restaurant, trying to look like we're thriving when I couldn't afford a Happy Meal, let alone whatever expensive nonsense was on this menu.

I glance at the menu prices, and I swear, I almost passed out right there. They're charging the price of a used car for a bowl of pasta. So, naturally, the panic sets in. My internal monologue? "Abort mission. Find a way out. Do not order the £40 salad." But of course, instead of being a normal person and admitting defeat, I had a brilliant idea. And by "brilliant," I mean "horrifically stupid."

So there I am, scanning the table like some kind of broken Sherlock Holmes, when I spot it—a piece of broken glass. Now, most people would think, "Oh, broken glass, let's avoid that." But no, not me. My brain goes, "This... this could be my ticket to a free meal!" Because, apparently, desperation makes you forget how glass works.

Jackie has no idea what I'm about to do. If she did, I'd probably be telling this story from the afterlife. Anyway, I casually slip that little shard of glass into my food when no one's looking. Yes, I actually did this. This is real life. Then, like an Oscar-worthy actor, I take a big, dramatic bite of food and pretend to find the glass in my mouth.

Now, if this story ended there, I'd just be mildly embarrassed. But no, it gets worse. WAY worse. As I'm doing my whole "Oh no, glass in my food!" routine, I actually cut my mouth on the real glass I just shoved in there. Because, of course, I did.

So, I'm sitting there, bleeding, like, "Great job, idiot. You've just glassed yourself for a free meal." The waiter rushes over, sees my face looking like a crime scene, and freaks out. Next thing I know, the manager is at our table, apologising like he's responsible for my terrible life choices. And then—the moment of triumph—he says, "Don't worry, your entire meal is free."

Not just for me. For everyone. Yup, I've just won everyone a free meal... at the cost of my face. My friends are practically popping champagne, toasting me like I'm some kind of genius, all while I'm sitting there trying to smile through the literal shards of glass stuck in my gums. I couldn't even eat the free food because, surprise, my mouth was too busy bleeding like a faucet.

But wait, it gets better! After everyone finished their delightful, free meal, I had to excuse myself to go to the hospital to get the glass removed from my mouth. That's right. I had to explain to the doctor why I had glass in my mouth. Try sounding smart after that conversation.

And here's the kicker: Should I have told Jackie the truth about my idiotic stunt? Absolutely not. Do I have a death wish? No, thank you. I kept my mouth shut (well, after they stitched it up), because I might be dumb, but I'm not suicidal. So, Jackie, if you're reading this... surprise! Love you!

Moral of the story? Never, EVER put glass in your food. Just pay for the overpriced pasta, or better yet, stay home and eat bread and water It's cheaper, safer, and you won't have to explain to your wife why you needed stitches for a free dinner

Chapter 36: How I'm Still Standing (Somehow)

I know what you're thinking. After reading about all the disasters, near-death experiences, and downright ridiculous situations I've gotten myself into, you're probably thinking, "This can't all be real." But let me tell you—it absolutely is. Every single thing I've written happened. And trust me, sometimes I can't believe it either.

How did I survive? I honestly have no idea. There must be some guardian angel up there working overtime because, by all rights, I should have my own reserved seat in the ER. Somehow, I'm still here, living to tell the tales (and probably embarrass myself all over again in the process).

And it's never-ending! Take this for example: I play squash to stay fit—great idea, right? Except somehow, I managed to run straight into the wall at full speed, knocking myself completely unconscious. I woke up to people standing over me, probably wondering how someone could mess up a game of squash that badly.

That's just me—disasters don't wait for the big moments; they come for the everyday ones, too.

At this point, I've stopped asking why these things happen and started embracing the fact that they just do. My life is basically a comedy of errors, and somehow, I'm still here to laugh about it... even when it hurts!

Carry on reading—you won't believe what's next!

Chapter 37: The Honeymoon Shenanigans: What Could Possibly Go Wrong?

Ah, my honeymoon—what could possibly go wrong, right? Well, considering it's me, that's a pretty stupid question. We booked a trip to Pescara, in the south of Italy—a beautiful place, by the way. As soon as we arrived, we checked in and decided to take a romantic walk. Naturally, as any grown man-child would, I spotted an amusement arcade. And of course, I had to go in. Jackie, my lovely, ever-patient wife, was not thrilled. She was hungry, but there I was, eyes wide, like a kid in a candy store.

Then, something magical caught my eye—bat and ball. Not the kind you'd play in a park, no. This was the prehistoric granddaddy of video games. No Xbox, no Nintendo back then—just this pixelated marvel with two bats, one on each side of the screen, and a ball bouncing back and forth. The bats moved up and down, and the game sped up the longer you played. Absolute edge-of-your-seat stuff! As they say, "small things please small minds," and let me tell you, I was thrilled.

Jackie, ever the practical one, says, "Let's eat first, then you can come back and play your little game." Yeah, she's the smart one.

Off we go, grab some chicken in a basket, and all I can think about is getting back to that arcade. I was like a man on a mission—Arcade Quest 1978. And then... there it was, looming 100 feet ahead, glowing like a beacon of joy. What could possibly go wrong? Oh, you're about to find out.

I start sprinting towards it. I'm flying, full speed, tunnel vision locked in. I'm almost there. And then... I ran into a giant glass wall. Like, not just any glass—this glass was practically invisible. I ricochet off it like I'm in a live-action cartoon. I hit it so hard I might as well have sent my soul into another dimension. I'm airborne, flailing through the air like a ragdoll, chicken going one way, dignity going the other

On the other side of the glass was this old guy, maybe 70, standing there, looking at me with wide eyes, like he was about to have a heart attack. Meanwhile, I'm laid out on the pavement, dazed, wondering if anyone got the number of the truck that just hit me.

And Jackie? Oh, Jackie. She strolls over, takes one look at me sprawled out like roadkill, and just shakes her head like, "Yup, this is my life now." Not a word. Not even a flicker of surprise. She's married to me, after all—she knew what she was signing up for.

Moral of the story? Always keep your eyes open for invisible glass... and maybe don't prioritise arcade games over dinner on your honeymoon!

Chapter 38: The Casino and the Toilet: What could possibly go wrong?

Alright, let me take you through one of the most ridiculous (and hilarious) moments of my life. Honestly, things just happen to me. I can't explain it. What could possibly go wrong, right? Yeah, you'd think I'd learn by now that's a terrible thing to say.

So, Jackie and I are headed out for a night at the casino with some friends (and yes, believe it or not, I do have friends, though after this night, I'm surprised they stuck around). It's one of those fancy casino nights—subsidised meals, a little gambling money thrown in. You know, the works. Sounds great, right? What could go wrong? Well, if you've met me, you know everything could go wrong...

We get there, and before I can even think about food, nature calls. Desperately. I tell Jackie, "Sign me in! I'll be right back!" and sprint off to the nearest bathroom like it's the Olympics. I burst through the door, not thinking twice. But after about a minute, something starts to feel... off. I'm hearing conversations that are suspicious... feminine. Women chatting about makeup, relationships, and who's dating who. That's when the light bulb goes off: I'm in the ladies' room.

I'm stuck in this cubicle, absolutely mortified, listening to these women chat about their lives, and all I can think is, "Jackie's going to murder me when she finds out." Not to mention, if the bouncers catch me in here, I'm pretty sure I'll get thrown out of the casino headfirst. Oh, and did I mention I'm starving? Two hours in a bathroom stall, and I missed the meal. Life's a party.

So, there I am, crouched in a cubicle for what feels like an eternity, too scared to move. After an hour and a half, things finally start to quiet down. I stand on the seat and peek over the top—like some sort of toilet ninja—and thank the heavens, it's empty! I make a mad dash for the door, praying no one sees me. I swear I've never moved so fast in my life.

I finally made it out, and of course, everyone's already finished eating. I try to explain the situation to Jackie, but she just gives me that look. You know, the "you're an idiot and we both know it" look. Yep, back in the doghouse again.

Moral of the story? Apparently, I'm not even safe to go to the bathroom in public. You'd think that'd be a basic life skill, but here we are.

Chapter 39: The Day My Brother Let Me Near a Brand New Van (It Didn't End Well)

Where do I even begin? With me, every day's an adventure. Nothing ever goes smoothly—especially when I'm working for my family. This time, my brother Bentley roped me into delivering a huge double-glazed unit down south. Now, you'd think after my many mishaps, my other brother Morris would've warned Bentley. But hey, I guess Bentley thought he'd give me a chance to prove myself. Poor guy. He had no idea what he was in for.

So, the day begins: sunny, perfect, birds singing—it's the kind of day where you just know things are about to go wrong. I was handed the keys to a brand-new, shiny blue van. Not ours, of course. No, this van was borrowed from the fitters. What could possibly go wrong? (I really need to stop saying that.)

My co-pilot for this adventure was Adrian, someone I'd never met before, which should've been the first red flag. About an hour into the trip, everything seemed fine—until I heard a noise. A kind of low rumble, like the van was growling at me. Naturally, I ignored it. We were in the middle of nowhere, cruising along the motorway, so I figured it was nothing. But then... THERE'S A BLOODY BIG BANG!

Adrian, wide-eyed, shouts, "What the hell was that?!"

Suddenly, the van gave up on life. I mean, no engine, no power, not even a wheeze. It was like the van just said, "You know what? I'm done with this." So, we coast to the hard shoulder in silence, and I'm thinking, "Okay, that's not too bad," until I look up and see flames coming out of the front.

Adrian's flapping his arms like a demented bird, screaming, "We're on fire!" Meanwhile, I'm just sitting there, calm as ever, and thinking "Well, of course. Because why wouldn't the van be on fire? This is my life."

We scrambled out of the van like it was about to explode, which—honestly—I half expected. Half the van was on fire, and the other half? Still in perfect condition, which was not a comforting thought because all four tires were now merrily ablaze. And here I was, blaming the fitters for lending me a van without a fire extinguisher. (Okay, fine, maybe I should've noticed something was wrong when the dashboard looked like a Christmas tree of warning lights, but that's neither here nor there.)

No mobile phones back then, no RAC membership. Well, I didn't have one. Why would I? And the nearest phone box? Felt like it was a thousand miles away—because, of course, why wouldn't it be? So, after what feels like a cross-country hike, we finally stumble upon one of those emergency phones on the motorway, like we've just discovered an ancient relic.

I grab the phone, praying it works, and dial Bentley. Because, you know, calling my brother for help has always gone so well before.

"Bentley, the van broke down."

"Where are you?"

"How the bloody hell should I know? We're in the middle of a field next to the motorway!"

"What field?! There is a number on the phone box?"

"Uh, 472-8-something…"

"How the hell am I supposed to know where that is? You think I'm psychic?!"

"Maybe the RAC will know?" I say, trying to sound like I actually have a plan.

"Well, that's cute," my brother replies. "We're not in the RAC."

"Not in the bloody RAC?! Brilliant. So what's the plan, then? You want us to push this flaming heap of metal back down the motorway? Maybe we'll hitch a ride with the bulls while we're at it!"

As if things couldn't get worse, Bentley casually drops the bomb: "Oh, by the way, that window unit you're hauling? Yeah, it's a one-of-a-kind piece from a 1400s church. Worth more than you'll make in a lifetime. Oh, and it's irreplaceable."

Fantastic. Just what I needed to hear. What Bentley doesn't know is that precious, historic window? Yeah, it's currently a smouldering pile of glass confetti. I'm dead. I'll have to leave the country, change my name—maybe grow a moustache. Do you think Jackie will come with me? I mean, she might forgive a lot, but burning down a priceless church artefact might be pushing it.

Oh no, not again, I can't believe I've set fire to history. Why does this keep happening to me?!

As we waited for the RAC, Adrian and I decided to go for a stroll through a peaceful field. We saw a house. Maybe they have a phone. The sun was shining, butterflies were flitting about, and for a brief moment, it was... nice. "Look at those cows," I said. Adrian turns to me and says, "Those aren't cows... those are bulls."

The bulls charging straight at us. Have you ever seen a man jump a 30-foot fence in sheer terror? Because I did that day. Adrian practically flew over the fence while I clambered after him, wheezing with laughter and fear at the same time.

We eventually stumble across a farmhouse, looking like we've just survived a zombie apocalypse. Thankfully, the fitters were in the RAC (because of course they were), so we used the phone and called my brother. After what feels like an eternity—seriously, I think I aged 10 years—they finally show up with a trailer to haul away what can only be described as the crispy, charred skeleton of a van.

The guy takes one look at the van, then at me, and I swear he was trying to figure out if I was part of the fire. I just gave him a nod like, "Yep, this happened. You're welcome."

And the next day? Oh, I never worked for my brother again. I think we both silently agreed I'd caused enough damage to last several lifetimes. I mean, he didn't say anything, but his expression screamed, "Please, for the love of all that's holy, stay far away from my business."

But hey, at least I got a killer story out of it... and a lifelong fear of bulls. Because, you know, why not throw that on the list of things I now avoid?

Oh, and I did tell Jackie. And what did she say? Exactly what you're thinking: "You did WHAT?!" Followed by, "How are you not in prison?"

Chapter 40: Jackie Always Said 'What Could Possibly Go Wrong?'... And Boy, Did I Prove Her Wrong!

I have to share something with you, and I say this with tears in my eyes. Every story I write, every memory I relive, even though she's no longer here, somehow brings me closer to her. It's like she's right beside me, smiling, listening to me just like she always did. We shared an incredible life together—one filled with laughter, love, and moments I wouldn't trade for the world. Not a single one.

She had this way of making even the most chaotic moments feel like they were meant to happen, like they were part of the grand adventure we were on together. No matter what I was going through, she listened. She listened to all my stories—every ridiculous mishap, every little victory, and every moment that made my life feel so full of meaning. And even now, as I write these stories down, I can feel her presence, like she's still here, sharing in the memories that made our life together so special.

I wouldn't change a single moment of it. Not one. Because every moment with her made my life worth living.

Looking back on my life, I realise it's been nothing short of a magical adventure—filled with twists, turns, and the kind of moments that take your breath away. I've been blessed beyond measure. I've loved and lost some truly beautiful souls, but their presence remains with me always. My five incredible children have brought me more joy than I ever could've imagined, and now, with three wonderful grandchildren, my heart feels fuller than ever. Every day feels like a new chapter in this amazing journey, and if I'm being honest, the best part is that it's only just beginning.

Enough with the sadness! Let's get back to the funnier side of life, because honestly, that's what life is—one big, ridiculous adventure! If you're not tripping over something, setting something on fire (accidentally, of course), or finding yourself in situations that make you wonder, "How did I even get here?" then are you really living? Life's too short not to laugh at the chaos, right?

Chapter 41: The Great Mouse Hunt: A Night to Remember

Looking back on my life, it's been a journey packed with surprises—moments so full of laughter they bring tears, and others so heavy they leave a lasting ache. Every day has felt like a unique chapter, filled with new lessons from the universe. It's as if life itself has been teaching me, leading me through this incredible, sometimes unexpected, adventure.

One of those memories stands out—a night with my two boys, Josh and Zak, when they were about six. It was around 7 p.m., an ordinary evening in our kitchen, where we were outnumbered by pets: two cats, two dogs, and the unpredictability that came with them. Ellie, our sleek black cat, had a habit of surprising us with "gifts." And on this particular evening, she decided it was my lucky day. With all the elegance of a cat queen, she dropped a still-wriggling mouse right at my feet.

And just like that, chaos erupted. The three of us sprang into action, slamming the kitchen door shut to keep our tiny intruder contained. It was like a scene from a comedy movie—Operation Mouse Hunt was officially underway. Josh, Zak, and I chased that little mouse all over, peeking under every cabinet, opening every cupboard.

The boys were fully in character, giggling and gasping, treating it like the biggest mission of their lives. And did I mention it was 7 p.m.? Not exactly what I had planned for a quiet evening!

That mouse was a little escape artist, darting out of reach every time we thought we'd cornered it. Meanwhile, Ellie sat back, watching us like a bemused queen, clearly wondering what all the fuss was about.

Now, every time I remember that night, I can't help but smile. It was one of those beautifully absurd moments that stitch themselves into the fabric of your heart.

I realise now that it wasn't really about the mouse; it was about the laughter, the teamwork, the way we three became partners in a ridiculous little adventure. Life has a way of turning the simplest moments into the best memories, the kind that stick with you that make the journey feel richer and fuller.

So let me tell you how it all went down. Time flew by in the madness of it all, and suddenly, its 2 a.m.—would you believe it? We still hadn't found that ridiculous little mouse! By this point, I was more worried that it had found itself a cosy corner, started a family, and planned to settle rent-free.

We kept searching, determined not to let it win. I was digging through every corner, pulling out anything that could possibly hide a mouse. I reached under the sink, took everything out, and finally, I picked up a vase sitting under there. Just as I was about to move on, I noticed my boys, Josh and Zak, both pointing at me with wide eyes. Confused, I looked down at the vase in my hands—and there it was, the mouse itself, peering over the edge, looking right back at me.

For a moment, we just stared at each other, like two characters in a cartoon. And then, I did the only thing that made sense: I screamed, dropped the vase, and jumped onto a kitchen chair like a cartoon character fleeing for their life! The vase shattered on the floor, and that little mouse? Gone—vanished into the shadows again. To this day, we never did find that clever little creature.

Years later, we remodelled the kitchen, and when we pulled out the old cooker, there it was—a little nest tucked right beside it, complete with a tiny bed. It looked like our guest had indeed moved in, maybe even raised a family, rent-free and entirely undisturbed. I like to think they're still around somewhere, living a cosy life in the walls. And that's okay by me. I hope they're nice and warm, wherever they are.

Chapter 42: The Great Poo-tastrophe: Josh and Zak's Two-Minute Masterpiece

Here we are once again with Josh and Zak, those two unforgettable little munchkins! This story takes us all the way back to when they were only 13 months old—tiny, curious, and full of surprises. I still remember the shock and wonder of that moment; I could hardly believe what unfolded right before my eyes. It's a memory that feels as vivid now as it did then!

Picture this: It's a peaceful morning. Jackie's out, so I'm left in charge of Josh and Zak, our two little cherubs. They'd just woken up, sitting in their cots with their nappies on, looking like tiny angels who couldn't possibly get into trouble.

Just as I'm about to change them, there's a knock at the door. The postman. I think, No problem, I'll just pop downstairs real quick. Two minutes. Two. I grab the mail, smile politely, say "Thanks," and head back upstairs. But as I open the door to their room, I stop dead in my tracks.

Oh. My. God.

In the space of two minutes, my sweet, innocent babies had transformed their room into a war zone. The walls? No longer white. They were a lovely shade of poo-brown, covered in... handprints? Streaks? Full-on abstract murals. They'd peeled off their nappies like they were shedding a bad outfit and used them as paintbrushes. Picasso? No. Poo-casso.

I looked over at their cots, but wait—there were no cots! Somehow, these one-year-olds had flipped them. Not tipped, not knocked over, but full-on flipped like they were trying to escape baby jail. And standing proudly in the middle of this poo-pocalypse were Josh and Zak, grinning like little maniacs, hands covered in brown smears up to their elbows. They looked like two mini wrestlers who'd just won a championship match in a mud pit.

And then, of course, there was the wardrobe. They'd somehow managed to open it, yank out every piece of clothing, and decorate it with their new "paint." My laundry! My once-fresh clothes now looked like they'd been used to wipe down a swamp.

I felt my soul leave my body. How? How could two toddlers create this much chaos in two minutes?! I stood there, caught between laughter and tears, knowing Jackie would be home soon and I'd be the one explaining the "modern art" in the nursery. I swear, I almost turned around and ran. Just me, the postman, and a one-way ticket to freedom.

But instead, I took a deep breath, rolled up my sleeves, and dove into the mess, making a mental note to invest in very secure baby onesies—and maybe a lock on the wardrobe.

I could never keep anything from Jackie, and honestly, I can't even imagine what she's going to say when she walks through that door. The second she sees the "artwork" smeared on the walls, the cots flipped over, and the clothes tossed around, she's probably going to freeze, eyes wide, processing the chaos.

Then she'll turn to me with that mix of disbelief and the tiniest smirk and say something like, "So... did you guys redecorate? Or is this some kind of modern art experiment gone horribly wrong?"

And as I stumble over an explanation, she'll definitely give me that classic look, holding back laughter, saying, "You had ONE job!"

Jackie took one look at the chaos, and her smirk turned into a full-blown laugh. She shook her head, pointing a finger at me. "I was right! One job!" she said, grinning like she'd known this would happen all along. "Told you!"

Chapter 43: Here we go again: The Time I Hijacked a Stranger's Car

Oh no, not again! So, picture this: it's a freezing winter's day, and, as usual, I'm running around like a headless chicken. Jackie suddenly yells, "We're out of nappies! You need to get some NOW!" Because, of course, when you've got five kids, running out of nappies is a full-scale emergency. Meanwhile, I'm already late for an appointment and in full-on chaos mode.

We've got a Nissan Serena, an eight-seater because, let's face it, with five kids, we basically run a mobile circus. Oh, and it's red—bright red. Remember that detail. This is one of those "you have to be kidding me" moments where the universe is like, "Let's mess with him a little more, shall we?"

I tear off to the shops, dash into the chemist, grab the nappies, and sprint back to the car. I jump in, sit down, and think, Wow, the car's never looked this clean! I mean, the dashboard's spotless! Then, out of the corner of my eye, I see something I didn't expect—a woman, sitting in the passenger seat, as white as a ghost.

Without thinking, I burst out, "WHO THE BLOODY HELL ARE YOU?!"

She looks at me, completely speechless, eyes wide with pure terror. That's when it hits me: I'm in the wrong car. Yep, wrong bloody vehicle! I quickly glance around and spot my car, two spaces over, staring back at me like, "Really, mate?"

So, naturally, I try to play it cool. I turn to this poor woman, who's probably having a nervous breakdown, and say, "Oh, terribly sorry! That's my car over there."

She doesn't say a word. Just sits there, frozen, probably questioning every life decision that led her to this moment. Meanwhile, I leg it back to my own car, get in, and speed off faster than you can say "awkward," hoping she doesn't start screaming.

I couldn't wait to tell Jackie. And what do you think she said?

"You did WHAT?!"

Chapter 44: The Hill Start from Hell: How I Nearly Got Flattened by a Runaway Car

I get it, life happens. But seriously, how is it even possible that all these things happen to me? So, there I was, on a gorgeous autumn day—clear blue sky, roof down on my 1360 convertible, blasting the Carpenters on my eight-track stereo (yeah, I'm that cool). I'm driving up Yew Tree Road toward Menlove Avenue, and for those of you not from Liverpool, let me paint the picture—it's a steep hill. What could possibly go wrong on such a beautiful day? Everything, my friend. Absolutely everything.

So, there I am, cruising along, about 150 yards from the traffic lights, feeling good, when all of a sudden—WHAM! A car coming down the hill from the other side smashes into a lamp post. I slam on the brakes just in time to see the lamp post snap into three pieces, and one of those giant metal chunks misses me by an inch. I mean, I was about to become a human pancake.

Naturally, I get out of the car, ready to confront the driver. I'm imagining this big, dramatic moment where I say, "What the bloody hell were you thinking? You nearly killed me, you bloody idiot!" But nah, I didn't say that. I look inside the car and—wait for it—there's no driver. No one. I'm standing there thinking, "Am I in an episode of The Twilight Zone?"

I look up the road, and there's this crowd of about twenty people, all sprinting after the car. Turns out, the poor woman driving had tried a hill start, slipped, and the car went rogue. She was literally chasing her own car down the hill, unable to catch it! I mean, at this point, the whole thing's like a comedy sketch.

When everyone finally reaches the scene, the woman's got blood pouring from her mouth—probably from biting her tongue while chasing a runaway car like she's in some kind of weird action movie. And out of nowhere, someone shouts, "I'm a doctor!" Great timing, right? I'm thinking, "Oh sure, now a doctor shows up. Where are you when I'm choking on my toast, huh?"

Then some other genius pipes up and says, "You need to move her car." I'm standing there like, "What do

I look like? The RAC? What's next, you want me to fix the engine while I'm at it?" At this point, I'm just standing there, shaking my head, thinking, "Yep, this is my life." Nearly flattened by a runaway car, and what do I have to show for it?

No one's asking if I'm okay, no one's checking to see if I need a therapy session, nothing! Just front-row seats to a live-action circus act. I swear, if there's a ridiculous disaster waiting to happen, I'm like a human magnet for it. Honestly, if there's even the slightest chance something absurd could go down, it's coming straight for me—like I've got "disaster waiting to happen" tattooed on my forehead!

Oh, and just so you know, I called the hospital to check on the lady—because clearly, I'm a saint, right? Turns out she's doing just fine, got patched up, and they sent her home. Meanwhile, I'm still emotionally recovering from nearly becoming a human speed bump, but hey, glad she's doing well! At least one of us made it out of that day without needing a therapist!

Chapter 45: My Life as the Universe's Punchline

As you've probably gathered after reading just a few of these wild episodes from my life, I'm starting to think I'm definitely not from this planet. I mean, seriously, normal people go about their day without ending up in full-blown slapstick comedy routines, right?

People go out for dinner, enjoy a nice meal, and maybe spill a little wine— big deal. Meanwhile, I'm out here dodging runaway cars like Mario Kart, getting trapped in toilets like I'm starring in a one-man sitcom, and almost booking a therapist because a lamp post nearly gave me a free lobotomy.

At this point, I'm convinced I'm some kind of cosmic joke. Like, maybe aliens plucked me from space, dropped me here for a laugh, and now they're up there watching like, "Look, he's at it again! Send in the runaway car!"

I mean, how else do you explain this? I can't just be unlucky. No, this has to be part of some intergalactic reality show called 'Watch This Guy's Life Fall Apart in Real Time!' Honestly, I'm half-expecting to find out there's a betting pool on what ridiculous thing's going to happen to me next.

Chapter 46: Speke Market Catastrophe

Where do I even start? And, yes, I have to say it: What could possibly go wrong? I really need to stop saying that. If you haven't already guessed, I'm a bit of a Del Boy. If something can go wrong, it absolutely will. I used to do the markets back in the day, and let me tell you, the adventures that came with it... well, they're enough to make anyone wonder if I've got some sort of "Disaster Magnet" badge sewn onto me somewhere.

You know the type—always out to make a quick buck, trying to sell anything that wasn't nailed down. But, like clockwork, every time I thought I'd struck gold, life would turn around, laugh in my face, and throw me straight into the deep end. Whether it was dodgy goods, stalls blowing over in the wind, or accidentally knocking over half the market while trying to set up, you name it, I've probably messed it up.

And it's not like small things go wrong. No, when I mess up, it's big. We're talking runaway chaos-level wrong. Honestly, sometimes I think the universe has a personal vendetta against me... or maybe it just likes a good laugh at my expense!

Well, back in the day, you could pretty much set up a market stall anywhere, and I mean anywhere. There was a market in Speke, Liverpool, and to get a decent spot, you had to arrive at an absolutely ridiculous hour—think 4 a.m.

Now, at this point, I'd only just started going out with Jackie. And let me tell you, Jackie was amazing. She was always trying to help us get on our feet, Alma amazing mum naturally, they both came along to help me with this crazy Sunday market gig.

This was right before Christmas, so we had a lot of stock. We were talking about enough stock to fill a small warehouse—because, you know, Christmas means people go bananas, right? It was the prime time to sell. So, we're there, it's pitch-black, freezing cold, and we're setting up like we're seasoned market pros (we definitely weren't).

I'm standing there trying to look confident, like I knew exactly what I was doing, even though half the time I was winging it. Jackie's there, all smiles, helping me unpack our stock, which, of course, was piled higher than Mount Everest.

Everything's set up, the stall is looking mint, and I'm thinking, "Right, this is it. We're about to make a fortune today!" You know, those famous last words before the universe steps in and says, "Oh, you thought this was going to go well? Hold my tea."

What could possibly go wrong, right? Well, let's just say... you're about to find out.

I said to Alma, Jackie's mum, "We need more stock." So, being the genius I am, I thought it was a great idea to nip to the wholesalers and buy more. One small issue—the stall was pitched around my car, like we'd built a fortress of Christmas tat.

No way was I moving it without causing a full market meltdown. So, naturally, I had to borrow Alma's car. Now, let me paint you a picture: Alma, lovely woman that she is, has this brand new yellow DAF. Mint condition. Absolutely pristine. And what does she do? She hands me the keys.

Why does this always happen to me?

She says, "No problem," with all the trust in the world. Huge mistake. I mean, the poor woman clearly has no idea what I'm like behind the wheel. I don't think she fully grasped that lending me a car is like giving a monkey a chainsaw—bad things are bound to happen.

Anyway, off I go, feeling a mix of excitement and dread, because let's be honest, I've got a track record. Picture this: It's the middle of winter, freezing cold, roads are icy, and here I am, behind the wheel of a banana-yellow DAF, trying to navigate icy streets like I'm auditioning for Ice Road Truckers. What could possibly go wrong, right? Well... brace yourself, because this adventure is about to take a turn.

So there I am, driving Alma's pristine, brand-new yellow DAF through Speke, which, let me tell you, is like navigating a maze designed by someone who really hates drivers. Every road seems to be blocked, so I'm turning left, turning right, trying to find my way.

Then, finally, I spotted an opening. Perfect, right? Except, oh wait, it's winter, and it's icy. Have you ever hit black ice? Well, things are about to get nasty, because of course, they are—it's me.

I hit the brakes, and guess what? The car doesn't stop. Nope, instead of making the turn, I sail right past it like I'm in some sort of icy car ballet. I'm skidding all over the place, and at this point, it's like I'm performing a scene from Dancing on Ice. Only problem? It's a cul-de-sac. On one side, there are six cars parked, and on the other side? Concrete bollards. So here I am, sliding down this street like a human-sized pinball, praying I don't smash into anyone's car.

By some miracle, I miss all the parked cars, and just when I think I might be in the clear—BAM! I hit one bollard. Then two. Then three, four, five, six bloody bollards. It's like I'm collecting them as if it's some sort of sick game. I'm in total shock, heart pounding, hands shaking, trying to comprehend the absolute disaster that just unfolded.

I get out of the car, trembling, and take a look at the damage. And there it is—a perfectly shaped dent in this beautiful, mint-condition, yellow DAF that's practically winking at me. The car's four wheels are the only thing keeping it from tipping over completely. I'm standing there, thinking, "Oh my god, I've just written off a brand-new car that isn't even mine." Not to mention, I'm 99% sure I'm not even insured for this.

Then, out of nowhere, this woman who witnessed the entire debacle walks over as calm as you like and says, "Are you alright, love? Would you like a cup of tea?"

A cup of tea?! Are you serious? I've just turned a showroom-worthy car into a crumpled piece of modern art, and she's offering me tea like we're in the middle of some nice afternoon chat? I'm standing there, covered in stress and regret, and she's asking if I want a bloody tea.

I somehow manage to reply, "No, thank you," because, clearly, I've lost the plot. Then I get back in the car, praying it'll still start. By some miracle, it does. And now, I've got the joyous task of driving back to the market to tell everyone the good news.

So off I go, driving back to the market, feeling like I'm heading to my own execution. I'm thinking, "How is this day going to end? Will Jackie ever speak to me again? And what on Earth is her mum going to say?" I had this crazy idea in my head to tell them the car was stolen and some vandals just happened to beat me up, and I heroically tried to stop them. But no, I decided to go with the classic "It wasn't my fault, it was the weather" excuse. Because, let's be honest, blaming Mother Nature is my best shot at survival.

I finally get back to the market, park the car with the massive dent facing away from the stall, hoping no one would notice the giant crumpled mess that used to be a mint-conditioned car. I get out, trying to look as casual as possible, and Jackie says, "Wow, you were quick! No traffic?" Oh, no traffic, alright. I nearly gave myself a heart attack! I felt like saying, "No, babe, just me turning the car into a sculpture exhibit while playing bumper cars with six bollards. No big deal!"

Then she looks at me, all concerned, and says, "You alright? You look like you've seen a ghost."

I think, "A ghost? You think?" I just had a near-death experience in a runaway ice-skating car! So, I take a deep breath and blurt out, "Uh... I had a bit of an accident with the car. Let me show you."

Jackie's mum walks over to the car, takes one look at the damage, and—brace yourself—she says, "Don't worry about the car. That can be repaired. You're more important."

I'm standing there, absolutely floored. Wow, amazing. But before I could fully appreciate that I wasn't getting disowned on the spot. Jackie, bless her, didn't speak to me for hours. Not until I finally cracked a joke and made her laugh.

And just like that, we were good again. Moral of the story? Always be funny enough to distract from a total car disaster... and maybe avoid black ice while driving someone else's brand-new car!

Chapter 47: The Great Gear Disaster: How I Nearly Destroyed a Car, My Wallet, and My Relationship

Oh, you are not going to believe this one. Disaster after disaster—it's like my life is some sort of cosmic joke. So, I didn't mention before, but Jackie, being the superstar she is, had just landed a role in the last series of The Liver Birds. Fancy, right? Only problem? She had to go to London for filming, and instead of doing the sensible thing—taking a train or a plane—we decided to drive. Why? Because clearly, I don't make good life choices, and apparently, the universe is in on this joke too.

We set off, all prepared: food in the car, tank full of petrol, the radio blasting tunes. I'm cruising along, 150 miles in, feeling like I've got this road trip thing down. Fifth gear, foot on the gas, everything's smooth sailing. But then—why does this always happen to me—I realise something's a bit off. You see, fifth gear and second gear are way too similar in this car. They're practically next-door neighbours. So, there I am, thinking I'm in fifth, cruising at 70 miles an hour, and feeling like a legend. But no. Oh no. I've been blasting down the motorway in second gear for a full hour like some kind of lunatic.

And, of course, I'm totally oblivious to the engine roaring like a lion on Red Bull. I mean, who listens to the engine when you've got 70s rock blaring? The gauges? Who checks those? Big red flag? Nah, let's just ignore that.

Then, BANG! A bloody big bang. The kind of bang that makes you think the car just exploded into a million tiny pieces. Jackie screams, "WHAT HAVE YOU DONE?!" like I've just personally dismantled the engine with my bare hands. And let me tell you, the drama is real.

We're smack in the middle of the motorway, and the car just gives up on life—no power, no nothing. It's like the car decided it had enough of my nonsense and said, "I'm outta here."

Can you picture it? Me, gripping the steering wheel for dear life, just praying we don't end up as a headline. And I'm lucky—I mean so lucky—that I'm coasting into the slow lane. Because otherwise, we're talking full-blown disaster, with me probably becoming a hood ornament on someone else's car.

Jackie? She turns to me, and those eyes—oh, those eyes—they could've set fire to the car faster than the smoke pouring out of the engine. You know the look. The kind that could murder you without a single word.

The kind of look that makes you question every decision you've ever made in your entire existence. And I'm sitting there, thinking, "Great. Here we go again. Another day, another disaster. Just my life on repeat!"

So, there we are, stranded on the motorway with smoke billowing from the engine like we're in a Fast & Furious movie gone wrong. And of course, no RAC. Why would I have the foresight to get roadside assistance? Genius move, right?

So, I figure, "No problem, I'll call David. He's bound to have an RAC card, right?" Wrong. David, the one guy who I'm banking on to save us, doesn't have an RAC card either. Fantastic.

Jackie, by this point, is not impressed. She's giving me that look like she's one deep breath away from pushing me into oncoming traffic. But David, being the hero he is, says, "Don't worry, mate, I'll come down and tow you home." Great! Problem solved. Or so I thought.

Three hours later—THREE HOURS—David finally rocks up, and he's not in some normal car with a tow rope, oh no. He shows up in a bloody big truck with a trailer. It's like he's about to rescue a tank, not my poor, destroyed Serena. I'm thinking, "Alright, at least we're going to make it home," but inside, I know—this is going to cost me more than just money.

So we finally got home, and I got the car to the garage. The grand total? Over three thousand pounds to fix the carnage I'd created. Yep, the kind of bill that makes your soul leave your body. And of course, Jackie gives me that look. You know, the one that says, "You're lucky to be alive right now."

Now, here's the kicker—I never told Jackie the real reason the car gave out. That I was driving in second gear at 70 miles an hour for an hour straight. Because, really, what do you think she'd have said? I can picture it now: "You did WHAT?!" Probably followed by me sleeping in the car I just wrecked.

Moral of the story? If you're going to drive like an idiot, at least get the RAC first.

Chapter 48: My Auntie and Uncle Nearly Had a Heart Attack

Well, here we go again—what could possibly go wrong? I'm honestly sick of saying that because, trust me, with my track record, everything can and does go wrong. Let me take you back: when my mum passed away, I ended up moving in with my auntie. It was supposed to be for two weeks... but, of course, that two weeks magically turned into eight years. Yep, eight whole years of misadventures, chaos, and everything in between. But that's a story for another time—when I'm feeling brave enough to dive deeper into that particular chapter of my life!

Alright, so my uncle trained me to be a welding engineer. Well, not that uncle—this was my other uncle. But let's get back to the real story here: It was back in the day when you could still buy flat-pack kitchens from MFI and pretend you knew how to assemble them without losing your sanity or a finger.

One Saturday, my auntie decided it was my time to shine. She asked me to put together some kitchen units, drill them into the wall, measure everything, and then hang them up. Simple enough, right? Wrong. The pièce de résistance was three glass-leaded cabinets where she planned to display her priceless cut glass and bone china that had been passed down through generations. You know, the kind of stuff that's basically an antique roadshow's dream.

Now, before I even got started, my auntie gave me the look and said, "You will be careful, won't you?" Famous. Last. Words. How many times have I heard that in my life? Too many. And, of course, I replied with full confidence, "What could possibly go wrong? I'm an engineer now!"

Let me just clarify: I had been "an engineer" for two whole weeks. Two. I'd worked with metal for 14 days, and suddenly, I thought I was Bob the Builder. I'm practically a pro, right? Well, buckle up, because you already know where this is going.

So there I am, drilling, measuring, and screwing things into the wall like I'm a professional, feeling like an absolute legend. Everything was going perfectly. I even stood back, crossed my arms, and said to my auntie, "Look at that! It's amazing!" I mean, this is me we're talking about—surely my family has told her what I'm like by now. But hey, everything's solid, perfectly in place, and I'm in her good books. Nothing to worry about, right?

Fast forward to Saturday night. Me and my cousin are heading out, ready to hit the town and try our luck with the ladies. By the way, great night, in case you're wondering. Everything's going smoothly, and we roll back home around 1:00 AM. As we pull up, I notice something odd—the lights are on. All night long my ears started burning, and that should have been the biggest red flag in history.

We walk in, and guess who's waiting to greet us? My uncle and auntie. Both of them, arms crossed, faces like thunder. They don't even need to say anything. You just know something is horribly wrong. Then, with an eerie calmness, they tell me, "Go into the kitchen."

Now, let me tell you, I've seen horror movies that were less terrifying than that moment. I open the kitchen door, and there it is—my masterpiece, those bloody units I'd put up, had fallen clean off the bloody wall. But wait, it gets worse. Her prized bone china and cut glass? Yeah, the ones that have been passed down through generations like some kind of royal heirloom? Shattered. Everywhere. The kitchen floor looked like a war zone of broken antiques.

I'm standing there, mouth open, staring at the carnage. My auntie, who used to love telling everyone the story about how this bone china was her pride and joy, now has a brand-new story to tell—about how her nephew single-handedly wrecked her entire kitchen display.

Oh shit. Not again. What have I done to deserve this? Is the universe actively punishing me? What do I even say to her? What could she possibly say to me? If there was ever a time to dig a hole and bury my head in the sand, this was it.

Oh, you want to know what she said. Well, let me set the scene for you. I'm standing there, ankle-deep in shattered glass and priceless bone china, looking like a deer in headlights. My aunt walks in, takes one look at the carnage, and lets out this long, deep sigh—the kind of sigh that makes you feel like you've just shaved ten years off her life.

Then she looks at me, calm as anything, and says, "Well, I did say be careful, didn't I?"

That's it. No yelling, no tantrum—just pure, passive-aggressive disappointment that cuts deeper than any shouting ever could. Honestly, I would've preferred if she'd thrown a plate at me (not that there were any left). It was like being hit with a silent sledgehammer of guilt. And let me tell you, the "I told you so" was loud and clear, even though she didn't say it.

My uncle? Just shook his head, muttered something about "bloody engineers," and walked off. At that point, I was ready to dig my own grave in the backyard.

I stood there in total disbelief, staring at the wreckage like, "How the hell did those units fall? They were perfect!" Solid to the wall, or so I thought. Then it hit me like a ton of bricks. I said to myself, "That's what those wall plugs were for!" Yep, I'd completely forgotten to put the bloody wall plugs in the wall. You know, the one thing that actually keeps the units from crashing down like a disaster movie.

I'm standing there thinking, "I am such a colossal idiot." I might as well have stuck the units up with chewing gum and good vibes. Won't make that mistake again! (But knowing me, let's not rule anything out.)

As for telling my auntie? Yeah, no chance. This is going to stay my little secret. The units just "mysteriously" fell, right? No need to tell her it's because I forgot the most basic part of DIY. Let's just sweep this one under the rug... assuming I can find a broom that hasn't been broken by my catastrophic home improvement skills!

Chapter 49: Should I Still Ask for My Wages?

Back with my brother again—and yes, let's just say I've officially been banned from driving his van. I mean, what could possibly go wrong, right? (Okay, I really need to stop saying that.) But this time, I'm not anywhere near the van, just working in his shop on a freezing Saturday. And when I say freezing, I mean ice on the ground freezing. But hey, not my problem, right?

So, it's near Christmas, the most wonderful time of the year, and my brother is in full festive mode. Every year, he gives out these fancy Christmas gift boxes to all the businesses that helped him out. We're talking top-shelf stuff—expensive bottles of whisky, brandy, the kind of alcohol that costs more than my monthly salary. He's got about 50 bottles, all laid out, looking like the crown jewels of booze.

So, naturally, he asks me to take the tray of bottles and load them into the back of the van. "No problem," I say, confidently, because, you know, what could possibly go wrong? (Cue the universe laughing at me again.)

I step outside, tray in hand, feeling like a pro. I mean, how hard could it be? The next second, I step on a patch of ice. And when I say "step," I mean I glide across it like I've just joined a figure skating competition I didn't sign up for. The tray of bottles flies out of my hands in slow motion, like some kind of disaster ballet.

I'm flailing, arms in the air, while the bottles soar like they're auditioning for a spot in Cirque du Soleil. Then, with a crash heard around the world, they hit the ground, smashing into what feels like a million pieces. Expensive whisky and brandy and champagne pouring everywhere, like we've just opened a bar for ghosts.

And me? Oh, I don't just fall. Oh no. I do a full-on somersault, like I'm an acrobat in the circus, flipping through the air like I'm training for the Olympics. I land flat on my back, staring up at the sky, wondering what I ever did to deserve this.

As I lay there in a puddle of expensive booze and broken glass, all I can think is, "Well, guess I'm banned from the shop now, too."

Then came the big question: What the hell do I tell my brother? Do I just play dead, lay there in the mess, and hope someone comes out, finds me "unconscious," and takes pity on my pathetic soul? No, no, I had to be a grown-up, right? Do the honest thing. So I brushed myself off, tried to look as dignified as one can in a puddle of smashed champagne whisky and brandy, and walked back into the shop.

But let me tell you, I was this close to just bolting, sprinting away like some kind of booze-smashing ninja. But no, I marched in there, head held high (sort of), and said, "Good news and bad news."

My brother gives me that look. You know, the one that says, "Oh great, what have you done this time?"

So I go, "Good news? The van's totally fine." I pause for effect. "Bad news? The tray's in good shape too… but the bottles? Yeah, not so much."

He just stares at me, deadpan. "What did you do?"

"Slipped. Everything smashed. I even did a somersault! You should've seen it! I'm talking about Olympic-level gymnastics here!"

Did he ask if I was okay? Nope. Not even a blink of concern for his poor, acrobatic brother. All he cared about were the 50 bottles of liquid gold now soaking into the pavement. I'm standing there, covered in whisky and shame, like, "Mate, I did a somersault! For goodness' sake, that's got to count for something!" But no, all I got was, "You're banned from touching anything ever again."

Fair enough.

Imagine the look on my brother's face when I stroll up, all casual, and say, "So, about my Saturday pay..." I mean, come on, I risked life and limb! I didn't just work; I performed an Olympic-level somersault, turned the pavement into a whisky-tasting event, and somehow, by some miracle, didn't smash up the van. If that doesn't scream "dedicated employee of the month," I don't know what does!

But yeah, maybe I should bring a helmet next time... y'know, just in case he launches one of those broken whisky bottles at me. If there's a next time, that is. Let's be honest, I might be banned from Saturdays altogether!

Oh, I can just imagine what he said. He probably gave me that long, tired look—the one that says, "How are we even related?" And then, after a deep sigh, he probably said something like, "You want your what now?"

Followed by, "You've shattered £500 worth of whisky, turned the shop into an ice rink, and gave the pavement a booze shower... and you're asking for wages?"

And then, to really drive it home, probably something like, "You're lucky I'm not charging you for the clean-up!"

Honestly, if I survive this without being paid in mops and paper towels for the next month, I'll consider it a win!

Chapter 50: What Could Possibly Go Wrong? - The Chronicles of My Ridiculous Survival

Alright, let's get this straight—every single story I've written down actually happened. No exaggeration. To this day, I have no clue how I'm still walking around in one piece. It's like I've got some kind of cosmic guardian angel who's constantly face palming and muttering, "Not again..." And trust me, I've got a lot more stories up my sleeve that would make you think, "There's no way this guy is still alive." But, oh, I am. Barely. Every time I say, "What could possibly go wrong?" life looks me dead in the eyes, cracks its knuckles, and says, "Oh, you wanna see?"

Honestly, My life? It's like playing a never-ending game of Jenga, but instead of wooden blocks, it was whisky bottles, kitchen disasters, and slippery ice patches all stacked up and ready to topple. And just like a guy who keeps pulling out the wrong piece, I keep thinking, "This time, it's gonna stay up!" it always comes crashing down

So, what could possibly go wrong this time? Oh, you're about to find out, because the universe has me on speed dial for chaos, and I'm apparently always available! Buckle up, because my life is basically "America's Funniest Home Videos," but without the prize money—or any sense of dignity.

Chapter 51: The Cost of Keeping Me Away: A Financially Sound Decision

Where do I even begin? When I got married, I didn't have a job. Now, you'd think that would bother most people, right? Not me. I'm a tradesman, a welder by trade, and I figured I could always make a living somehow. But then, plot twist—my uncle sacked me just before I got married. Yep, you heard that right. My uncle. You'd think family would have your back, but apparently, they didn't want me to get married and decided to make life a bit more "challenging." It was like a family obstacle course designed to break me. But I didn't care—no way was I letting anyone talk bad about them. They're family, after all. But trust me, that's a story for another day.

So, fast forward. We got married, went off on our honeymoon—which, well, you already know how that adventure went. Had an amazing time, by the way, but let's get to the real drama: we get back from the honeymoon, and reality hits us like a brick to the face. How in the world are we going to survive? We'd blown all our money on the holiday. All of it. Every penny. And now, we're back at Jackie's mum's place. Not the worst situation, but let's just say privacy was a luxury we didn't have. You know what I mean. Trying to start a life while sharing walls with your in-laws? Let's just say, "Awkward" doesn't even begin to cover it!

It was like being on a permanent first date—only with your mother-in-law next door, ears pricked up like a hawk. Every creak in the floor, every whisper, and there's a sudden, "Everything alright in there?" We couldn't even look at each other without feeling like we were under surveillance! Honestly, I'm surprised we didn't end up drawing up visitation hours for the living room.

Oh, and did I mention I was only 24 when I got married? Yep, I tied the knot young, but honestly, I loved being married—maybe because I didn't really have anyone before Jackie. But you'll understand that part later in the book. Anyway, back to the story: no job, but hey, we were happy. And guess what Jackie did? No, no, don't jump to conclusions—she didn't leave me. She actually got me a job! Doing contract work at Pilkington Glass, the sheet works in St. Helens. First day on the job? I'm feeling like I've made it. I'm meeting all the characters, thinking, "This is a breeze."

Now, here's the kicker: we got paid weekly. My first wage packet? Hold onto your seat—three hundred and sixty-five pounds! Yeah, you heard that right—three hundred and sixty-five bloody pounds! I couldn't believe it. I was practically skipping home to tell Jackie, grinning like I'd just won the lottery. Let me remind you, when I worked for my uncle (the same one who sacked me), I slaved away 80 hours a week for a grand total of... wait for it... thirty pounds. THIRTY! For an 80-hour week! But hey, at least he taught me a trade, right?

So I rush home, give Jackie the money, thinking I'm the king of the world. I mean, she got me the job, so naturally, she deserved to know how much we were raking in. And what does she say? "What's yours is mine, and what's mine is mine." And here's the best part: being the dopey 24-year-old that I was, I actually thought she was right!

Can you imagine? There I was, handing over my hard-earned cash, while Jackie was just grinning like she'd pulled the ultimate heist!

Months go by without a hitch, and I'm thinking, "Maybe the universe has finally fallen asleep or found someone else to torment." Things are going too smoothly, which, for me, is always a red flag. Then, like a fool, I let those cursed words slip out of my mouth: "What could possibly go wrong?" Oh no. Not again. The second those words leave my lips, I know the universe has just rubbed its hands together and said, "Time to mess with this guy again."

So, it's a beautiful summer's day, and I'm at work, loving life. I'm like a metal doctor, learning new things every day. Feeling unstoppable, right? That's when the foreman walks up to me and says, "I need you to come with me." And in that moment, I should have known something was up. He leads me into this building that's about six stories high, and I'm thinking, "Okay, no big deal, just another day in the life of a welding wizard."

But oh, no, this is where things go off the rails. He points to this monster—a ten-foot by ten-foot, two-inch-thick steel plate, bolted together and running up all six floors of the building. And he wants me to weld it. I'm staring at this thing, and all I can think is, "Well, here we go. The shit's about to hit the fan."

Now, let me paint you a picture: inside this beast of a contraption is a thick layer of rubber, and attached to it are giant shovels carrying sand up six floors. The sand is then hauled across to another building where they make the glass. And if you don't know, St. Helens glass is massive—it's like the Ferrari of glassmaking. They transport this stuff like treasure.

So here I am, looking at this Frankenstein of a project, and I just know something's going to go horribly wrong. You don't need a crystal ball when you're me. The universe was just giving me a little break so I could be nice and rested for my next disaster!

So, the job seemed simple enough: weld some metal plates where the frame had worn down. Easy-peasy, right? I ask Dave, the foreman (lovely guy, by the way), "Is all the machinery off?" Without missing a beat, he goes, "Of course, mate, it's all off." Famous last words.

So there I am, doing my thing, welding these plates onto the frame, feeling like a proper expert. And, as usual, I mutter to myself, "What could possibly go wrong?" I really, really need to stop saying that.

About an hour in, I start hearing these loud, thundering noises coming from the frame. It sounds like a bloody freight train's about to burst through the wall. My first thought? "Oh, great, the machinery's turned on and I'm about to be turned into a human pancake." So I leg it up to Dave's office, bust in, and say, "Dave, is the machinery on?"

He looks at me like I've asked him if the sky's still blue and says, "No, Geof, it's all off. Why?"

"Well," I say, "I can hear a very concerning noise coming from the third floor."

So, we both make our way down there, and what do we see? The bloody frame is glowing red hot, with smoke billowing out of every possible crack and crevice. It's like a scene from Dante's Inferno. I'm standing there, staring at this glowing disaster, and then I look at Dave—expecting him to spring into action. Nope. He just freezes. Literally freezes. He looks at me, I look at him, and it's like we're in some kind of comedy sketch where no one knows what the hell to do.

Meanwhile, I'm thinking, "Well, there goes the easy job... and probably my career."

So, it's clear that I'm the one who's going to have to spring into action because Dave's still frozen like a deer in headlights. Meanwhile, the bloody frame is glowing like it's been possessed by the devil himself. Now, let me remind you, St. Helens Glass has its own fire brigade, so I smack the alarm button like I'm defusing a bomb, and I'm thinking, "They'll be here in no time, right?"

Wrong.

Thirty minutes go by. Thirty bloody minutes! The entire frame is now basically an inferno, and I'm standing there, thinking, "Are they having a tea break? A casual chat about the weather? What's next, they'll show up in their slippers?" At this point, I'm half expecting to see them roll in with scones and a flask of tea, casually asking, "So, what's the issue here, then?"

By the time they finally arrive, I've aged about ten years, and the frame looks like it's trying to audition for a role in the next Die Hard movie. Honestly, at this rate, I'm starting to wonder if I should've just put out the fire with a garden hose myself!

So, the fire brigade finally shows up, and instead of springing into action like you'd expect, they come up to me and ask, "How can we put it out?" I'm standing there, covered in soot, and thinking, "Why are they asking me? Aren't they supposed to know how to put out a bloody fire?" Then it hits me—they don't mean how to put it out, they're asking, "How do we even get in there to put it out?"

Brilliant.

So I explain, with all the patience I've got left, "We need to haul the hoses all the way up to the sixth floor." And who's helping them lug those hoses up six flights of stairs? You guessed it—yours truly. Then, of course, the lid of the frame is bolted down, so I've got to burn it off to get inside. By the time they finally get the fire under control, it was pitch black, and I'm standing there looking like I've just crawled out of a coal mine. I'm knackered, covered in soot, and barely holding it together.

Just when I think the nightmare is over, in walks Mr. Know-It-All, some engineer in a suit, strutting in like he's auditioning for The Apprentice. He takes one look at the scene and asks, "Who's responsible for this?"

Naturally, everyone points straight at me.

He glares at me, practically fuming, and says, "Do you have any idea what you've done? You've caused the first-ever total shutdown of St. Helens Glass production! Do you know how much this is going to cost?"

I'm standing there, absolutely exhausted, covered in soot from head to toe, and without missing a beat, I fire back sarcastically, "I really don't care, but I'm guessing it's not pocket change!"

"Oh, I'll tell you," he says, like he's been waiting his whole life for this moment. "Between £750,000 and £1,000,000 pounds."

I'm standing there, thinking to myself, "Well, that's slightly worse than the time I wrecked my brother's business... but hey, I guess I'm definitely moving up in the world!"

Now, I'm beyond annoyed at this point, because I've literally just helped save the place from burning down, and this guy is lecturing me like I started the fire for fun. So, I look him dead in the eye and say, "You bloody idiot! You want to know how it started. Inside that metal frame is a vacuum—pure oxygen. A spark touched the rubber belt, oxygen fuelled the flame, and the whole thing went up like a bonfire. Within seconds! That's why it happened, and you should've had a fire marshal with me in the first place. But you didn't, and now I'm covered in soot, so I'm going home!"

And with that, I walked out, got in my car, and drove home like I'd just survived the apocalypse.

When I got home, Jackie took one look at me—covered in soot, looking like I'd just crawled out of a chimney—and her face was priceless. She raised an eyebrow and said, "What on earth happened to you?"

So, I started telling her the whole saga—how the machinery went up in flames, how I had to help the fire brigade, how Mr. Know-It-All in a suit told me I'd cost the company nearly a million pounds.

And do you know what she said?

She just shook her head, smirked, and said, "Only you could go to work as a welder and come home looking like you've been moonlighting as a firefighter. Did you at least ask for a raise?"

She really made me laugh—Jackie always had a way of making me feel better, no matter what disaster I came home from. After I told her the whole story, she just grinned and said, "Only you could nearly burn down a glass factory and come out of it thinking you're the victim." We had a good laugh about it, and that was that... until the next morning.

Turns out, the whole fiasco made it into the St. Helens papers. And get this—they thought it was sabotage! I nearly choked on my tea reading it. Meanwhile, I'm thinking, "Sabotage? Nah, just me being my usual, clumsy self." Although, after calling that engineer a "f***ing idiot, I wouldn't be surprised if he tried to frame me. I mean, why not? I did call him out in front of everyone!

A week goes by, and I muster up the courage to go back in and get my wages. As I walk through the door, I brace myself, expecting security guards to come and escort me off the premises in case I accidentally set something else on fire. The foreman spots me and heads over, and I'm thinking, "Here it comes—my grand exit."

Instead, he hands me my wages and, to my shock, says, "Where've you been? We've got another contract for you."

Another contract! I nearly fainted on the spot. Turns out, at the hearing, when they mentioned my name, someone actually stood up and said, "Geof's accident-prone, but it's not his fault!" My reputation is saved... barely!

I was honestly standing there thinking, "Surely, it would be in everyone's best interest if they just paid me to stay away!" I mean, can you imagine the cost savings? No more fiery disasters, no more equipment meltdowns, no more accidental factory shutdowns! I'm practically a walking financial crisis.

If they're smart, they'll realise paying me a small fee to not show up is a solid investment! I'm starting to wonder if they've done the maths. Honestly, it makes you think—how much would they save just by keeping me off the premises? I might be the first person in history to get paid to not do their job!

Chapter 52: How I Nearly Turned a Welding Job into an Action Movie

So there I was, working at Pilkington's in St. Helens, three hundred feet up on scaffolding, welding away, thinking, "Ah, what a beautiful day—what could possibly go wrong?" Well, let me tell you, everything was about to go wrong.

Now, they'd given us harnesses for "safety." But these harnesses had a mind of their own. Every time you moved, they'd catch on something, and you'd end up flinging yourself off the scaffolding like you were auditioning for the circus. So, naturally, I decided to remove the safety device and go rogue. Smart, right?

So, I'm in my harness-free zone, happily welding, when I realise I'm running out of rods. I asked one of the guys to get me some, but then I thought, "Nah, it'll be quicker if I grab them myself." Now, we didn't walk down scaffolding like normal people—oh no. We swung from bar to bar, dropping down 14 feet at a time like chimps with a death wish.

So off I go, swinging down like some DIY Tarzan, dropping level by level, and finally, I hit the last floor... only for the entire thing to give way beneath me. Turns out, the planks were rotten right through, so I crashed through one floor, then the next, each time thinking, "Surely, this one will hold me." they didn't. I was dropping like a rock, busting through floors like I was in a human game of Snakes and Ladders, minus the ladders.

Somehow, as I'm plummeting, I managed to grab onto the scaffolding, dangling there like Indiana Jones after a really bad day, trying to wrap my head around the fact that I'm still alive. Not a scratch on me, but I've just turned five floors into sawdust.

Of course, I'm bracing myself for that crusty old engineer to come charging over and start his usual lecture. I'm sure he's thinking, "Oh great, the guy who caused a million-pound fire is back at it." But hey, you can't blame a guy for adding a bit of excitement to the workday, right?

And that, my friend, is how I nearly created a demolition derby on a scaffold—all for a handful of welding rods.

Now, you'd think they'd have learned their lesson after the last time—you know, when I nearly burned the entire place to the ground and racked up a small fortune in damages! But no, there I was, back on the job, as if they'd completely forgotten my first disaster. It's like they looked at my resume and thought, "Oh, this is the guy who set everything on fire? Yeah, he deserves a second chance!"

Chapter 53: £29,500 for a Luxury Rat Hotel

So, let me tell you about the disaster that is January 2024. I've had this gorgeous white Audi A5 convertible, barely 6,000 miles on it when I bought it—absolute baby, immaculate. For almost three years, it's driven like a dream. I'm talking luxury, the wind in my hair, the kind of car that makes you feel like a millionaire even when you're just going to the supermarket.

Then, boom—2024 arrives, and everything starts going downhill. I get in the car one morning, and suddenly it's like I'm at a bloody disco—flashing lights everywhere. Every warning light you can imagine, lighting up the dashboard like a Christmas tree. So, naturally, I call my son-in-law Richard, who has his own MOT station. I mean, what could possibly be wrong with it? It's basically brand new, right? (Oh no, I said it. I've learned now, saying "what could go wrong" is like asking the universe to smack you in the face.)

So, Richard pops the bonnet, and would you believe it—rats! Bloody rats had moved in and made my beautiful car their personal luxury condo. I'm standing there, jaw on the floor, while Richard is trying to hold in his laughter. They'd been chewing on the wiring like it was a bloody buffet!

My gorgeous car, reduced to a rat nest. You couldn't make this up.

Anyway, I ring the insurance company, and they casually ask, "Is it a write-off?" A write-off? For a few chewed wires? I nearly dropped the phone. I had to repeat myself, "No, mate, it's just the wires!" And they go, "Well, if it can't be repaired, it'll be a write-off." A write-off? For some rats doing their worst?

At this point, I'm imagining my precious Audi getting crushed into a cube because some rodents decided to have a party under the bonnet. So, I call Richard back, and we bring in an auto electrician, hoping for a miracle. The guy shows up, takes one look, and says, "Yeah, I can fix this. That'll be £375." Phew, right? Relief. He also throws in some life advice: "Keep it away from the bins."

Thanks, mate. Didn't realise I needed to keep my luxury car in a rat-free zone.

I immediately called the insurance to cancel the claim. Crisis averted. But here's the thing—something is telling me I need to get rid of this car. It's like the universe is having a laugh at my expense, playing games with me again. I mean, what's next? You won't believe it, but you know something's coming.

Stay tuned. Because if rats weren't enough, I'm sure the universe has another curveball with my name on it!

Now, I'm sitting in the car and the dashboard shows a problem with the gearbox. How is this even possible? The car's only done 14,000 miles! This thing's practically a toddler in car years!

The next day, I got in touch with the RAC. Nice guy Neil shows up. Super friendly, you know the type—comes in like everything's under control, making me feel like I haven't been cursed by the universe. He pops the bonnet, takes a look inside, and—would you believe it—the bloody rats have been at it AGAIN. This time, there's rat poop everywhere, like they've had a full-on festival under the bonnet. I'm standing there, in utter disbelief, like, really? What is this? Some kind of rodent revenge saga? First, they chew through my wires, and now they've decided to take a dump in my engine for round two!

Neil looks at me, trying to keep a straight face, while I'm about two seconds from throwing a tantrum in the middle of my driveway. Rats. Again.

So, naturally, I ring Richard. You can probably imagine what he said—something along the lines of, "What the hell are you feeding these rats? Caviar and premium wires?" He's laughing, I'm fuming, and the rats? Well, they're probably somewhere nearby, planning their next attack.

Honestly, at this point, I'm convinced these rats have a personal vendetta against me. What's next? Are they going to start driving the car too? I wouldn't be surprised if I walked out one day and saw them cruising down the street in my Audi!

Oh, did I mention I paid £29,500 for this car? Yeah, nearly thirty grand for what has basically turned into a luxury rat hotel. Seriously, all I've had are bloody problems. I'm convinced I should've just thrown the money into a bonfire and at least gotten some warmth out of it.

So, I call Richard again, and his first words? "Was the car parked by the bins?" Oh, brilliant, let's rub it in, shall we? Like I've set up a rat sanctuary in my driveway just to spice things up. Meanwhile, he's laughing so hard, I can practically hear him wiping away tears. I swear, he's loving this.

"Can't wait to tell Gema!" he says, like this is prime entertainment. He's in stitches, and here I am, out nearly thirty grand, and the closest thing to enjoying my Audi is being a rat landlord.

At this point, I'm half expecting these rats to send me rent checks or maybe throw me a housewarming party for the new wiring they've installed themselves. And Richard? Oh, he's loving every second, probably planning to make this the punchline at every family dinner for the next decade.

So, what now? Well, next up is the dreaded call to the insurance company to see if my precious Audi is going to be declared a write-off. Honestly, I feel like crying—actual tears. Picture it: me, curled up in a ball, rocking back and forth, whispering "Why me?" while rats somewhere are probably toasting to their victory over my once-beautiful car.

The worst part? It's like waiting for a judge to deliver the verdict: "Is it repairable or will it be sentenced to the scrapyard?" Only time will tell, but let's be real—given my luck, I'm fully expecting the universe to throw one last twist. Maybe the insurance guy will say, "Sorry, mate, we don't cover rodent revenge."

So yeah, let's just wait and see what fresh disaster is about to be delivered to my doorstep. Maybe the rats are drafting up a formal eviction notice as we speak

Chapter 54: The Window Sale That Turned Into a Muddy Meltdown: It's Not My Fault!

Alright, buckle up, because this one's a gem. So, I was selling windows at the time, and I had a 7 o'clock appointment. Middle of winter, absolutely bucketing down with rain, the kind where you need an ark, not a car. Anyway, I arrived early. The gentleman answers the door, says, "My wife's out, getting her hair done in town, but she'll be back shortly." Great, no problem. He makes me a cup of coffee, and we sit there chatting—really nice guy.

An hour goes by. No wife. Two hours. No wife. Three hours—still no wife. I did mention it was winter and pouring rain, right? The kind of rain that makes you reconsider every life choice you've ever made. I'm starting to wonder if she got lost or if I'm about to be part of some mystery show where the wife never returns.

Suddenly, the door slams open, and in walks the wife... and let me tell you, she looked like she had been dragged backwards through a mud bath, straight out of a horror film. Honestly, the look on her face would have sent Norman Bates running. Think "Psycho"—except she looked like the one that's already dead. Her hair? Absolutely ruined. Makeup? Gone. The fury? Unmatched.

She storms in, dripping wet, looking like she just survived a natural disaster, and her husband, bless him, goes, "Oh, love, where've you been?"

Where has she been? Oh, you should've seen the look on her face. She snaps back, "Where have I fucking been? Look at me!" And then, with all the cluelessness of a man who's about to get murdered, he goes, "I'll make you a nice cup of tea."

Cup of tea?! CUP OF TEA?! This woman has been rained on, stranded, and probably fighting off wolves at this point, and he's offering her tea. She fires back, "I've been waiting for you for three hours in the pouring rain! Had to get a taxi, it took over a bloody hour to find one!"

And then, here's the thing. The husband blinks, looks utterly confused, and says, "But you took the car."

At that moment, she turned as red as a beetroot. And I'm sorry—I couldn't help it. I burst out laughing. I know, I know, totally inappropriate, but I couldn't hold it in. And then, the husband starts laughing. Now we're both sitting there, howling, while she's standing there, drenched, fuming, and covered in mud.

"Oh my god, I DID take the car! Where the hell did I put it?"

Trust me, she wasn't happy. She looked at me like I'd just told her I'd sold the family heirlooms on eBay. I tried to explain—"Look, it's not lost exactly… it's just… temporarily misplaced"—but that only made it worse. I swear, if looks could kill, I'd be toast.

And here I am, trying to lighten the mood, saying, "Hey, at least you'll get some exercise when you walk around looking for it, right?" But nope, not a smile in sight. I'm telling you, I've seen happier faces in horror movies!

I can tell you one thing: after he laughed, that man was definitely not in the good books. I'm pretty sure if looks could kill, he'd be six feet under right now. She stared at him like she was plotting his slow, painful death, while he's still chuckling, oblivious to the fact that his life might be in immediate danger.

And the best part? This time, it definitely wasn't my fault! I'm just an innocent bystander, dragged into this muddy meltdown of a situation, and I suddenly realised... yep, I need to get the hell out of here. So I grabbed my coat, mumbling something like, "Uh, I think I'll just... leave you guys to... sort this out," as I backed out of the room, trying not to make eye contact with the furious woman.

I'm pretty sure that when I left, they had more than windows to talk about. I just hope the poor guy survived to see another day!

Chapter 55: A Journey Through Shadows: The Story I've Been Afraid to Share

Sometimes, life sweeps us onto paths we could never have anticipated, leading us through moments of joy and wonder, but also into depths of sorrow that linger far beyond their time. The story I'm about to share is one that I've often tried to lighten, framing it within the humour of life's little surprises. But there's a deeper truth here, a raw and aching sadness that has shadowed my heart since I was a child. Today, I feel I can no longer hide it behind smiles or keep it safely tucked away.

Writing these words, revisiting these memories, is something I have avoided for so long. The weight of them, the pain they carry, is a part of me—one that time cannot soften. It is a sadness I have carried quietly, one that will remain with me, etched into my heart, until my final moments. No matter how many years pass, the sorrow clings, ever present, like a wound that refuses to fully heal.

It has taken countless tears and sleepless nights to reach this moment, to summon the courage to lay bare this part of my soul. To share this story is to expose a vulnerability I've shielded, a sadness I've hidden from even myself at times. Yet, I feel that now, finally, is the time to let these emotions breathe, to let this story be known.

These words come from the deepest recesses of my heart, and as I write, I can only hope that I find the strength and clarity to express the enormity of what we went through. It is my sincere hope and prayer that sharing this story may bring some release, some small peace. And perhaps, through these words, others might understand the weight of this journey—a journey I will carry with me until I leave this world.

December 16th, 1999: The day that shattered us leaving us with a sorrow that time cannot touch.

December 16th, 1999—a date that is carved deep within us, a wound that remains raw and unhealed. It was the day our world was torn apart, the day that brought a grief so profound, so relentless, that it will stay with us as long as we live. To truly understand what this date means, we have to go back to 1996, three years before, to a time when life felt safe, untouched by the cruelty we never saw coming.

In 1996, like every year, Jackie went in for her routine mammogram. It was supposed to be simple, another routine check-up. But that day, everything changed. They found something. Just a shadow, a small lump. But in that instant, life as we knew it began to slip from our grasp.

There was a biopsy, and we clung to every bit of hope we had, praying, bargaining, begging for it to be nothing. But then the news came, cutting through us with brutal clarity: breast cancer. Jackie was only 41.

I will never forget the look in her eyes that day. A light in her dimmed, the warmth and brightness that defined her suddenly flickering. There was a rawness, a fear so deep and shattering that it almost hurt to look at her.

She looked as though she'd been handed a death sentence, as though her future had been taken from her in a single breath. In that moment, we lost part of her spirit, part of Jackie who was filled with laughter and joy. With a few words, the world had taken something precious from her—and from us all.

From that day forward, everything changed. Each day became a battle, a silent war against an enemy we couldn't see but feared constantly. Each moment became painfully precious, yet filled with dread. Jackie found a strength none of us could have imagined, but behind that strength was a sadness, a quiet terror that hovered in the air, even when no one spoke of it. We held onto her, onto each other, as the weight of uncertainty pressed down on us, breaking us little by little.

Jackie faced her diagnosis with a bravery that broke our hearts. She walked into every treatment with a quiet strength, enduring round after round of radiotherapy and chemotherapy—the treatments that were meant to save her.

But looking back now, with all that I've learned, a part of me aches, wishing she hadn't had to go through it all. If I could turn back time, I'd give anything to spare her that suffering. But back then, we didn't know; we only knew that this was the way forward, the path we were told could keep her with us.

Then came the mastectomy, a devastating blow that felt like the ultimate test of her spirit. Through it all, Jackie held her head high, even as she lost her hair, her strength, and her own familiar reflection in the mirror. Piece by piece, she watched parts of herself slip away. And yet, she fought on, holding steady, with a resolve that left us both inspired and shattered. There were days when her smile was brittle, her laughter thin, but she kept going. And finally, after what felt like a lifetime, the news came: she was in remission.

For a moment, we let ourselves breathe again, to believe that maybe the worst had passed. In those fragile, tentative months, we clung to each other, finding strength in every small victory, celebrating every day she was still with us.

We were willing to try anything to keep her safe, so we changed everything. Jackie began the Gerson Diet, a strict regimen we hoped would fight off any last shadow of cancer. It felt like our last stand, a final way to protect her.

We poured ourselves into every hopeful avenue, desperate to keep her with us, clinging to the smallest bit of hope like it was air itself. She endured it all, every painful day, every setback, not for herself, but for us— she wanted to stay with us, even though the battle wore her down more than words could ever capture. Jackie was the bravest soul I've ever known, and she gave everything to that fight.

But despite her courage, despite the unyielding spirit she carried through each gruelling day, the toll was heavy. And even as we clung to the idea of remission, that shadow of cancer, that unshakable fear, lingered over us, reminding us of how fragile hope can be, of how deeply painful it is to love someone so much and to realise that some things lie forever beyond our control.

Over those two years, the children were incredible. Everyone had a role, something to do, some way to contribute to Jackie's healing. The Gerson therapy was strict, unyielding. Every detail had to be just right— lemon and apple juices, countless glasses of fresh, organic juices each day. They embraced it all, determined to do whatever it took. For two years, we held to this path, clinging to hope. And then, 1999 arrived, and with it, the moment we'd been dreading.

Jackie started noticing pain in her back. At first, we tried to believe it was nothing, a passing ache. But she grew more concerned, and finally, she said she wanted to get it checked out, privately this time. We made an appointment at a private hospital in Wirral. I remember that day so clearly. We'd just returned from Sefton Park in Liverpool, walking along the path by the daffodils, where I kept reassuring her that everything would be fine. I wanted so badly to believe it myself.

When we got home, the phone started ringing. Jackie didn't want me to answer it. It rang six times, each ring heavy with dread. Then, there was a knock on the front door. She didn't want me to open it, but I did. It was the doctor, standing there with a sombre expression, words he didn't want to say. He told us an ambulance was on its way and that the situation was urgent.

They'd reviewed her CAT scan results immediately. Jackie's spine, they told us, was barely supported, hanging by a thread, ready to collapse at any moment. The cancer had returned, not quietly or subtly but with a vengeance. It had spread to her bones, her spine, mercilessly. They rushed her to Clatterbridge Hospital, and just a few days later, she came home, her body frail, her strength fading fast.

The weight fell off her so quickly; it was like watching her disappear right in front of us. I knew in my heart I couldn't let her die in a hospital. She needed to be at home, surrounded by the people she loved, in the place that held so many of our memories. And so, a week later, she passed away in our bed, peacefully, surrounded by love.

If ever I have known regret, it is at this moment. I carry it with me. When she'd gone for her mammogram the year before, they'd told us everything was fine. But the following year, they revealed something unthinkable: she'd had cancer for six years, undetected. If they had found it back then, perhaps she would still be here. It's a thought that haunts me, that replays in my mind. I would have given anything to save her, to change that outcome.

December 16th, 1999 marked the end of that fight. The day the battle we'd fought so fiercely came to a heart-breaking close. It left a void in us, an emptiness that no words could ever fill, and a sorrow that has rooted itself in our lives.

And although life goes on, although we have learned to live with the emptiness, that day remains—etched in us as a reminder of everything we lost, of the light that was stolen too soon, of a sadness that has woven itself into the very fabric of who we are.

Jackie's spirit, her laughter, her love—they live on in our hearts, but the pain of her loss will forever be a part of us. December 16th,

1999 is not just a date; it is the day our world shattered, leaving us with a sorrow that time cannot touch.

In the end, she was taken from us far too soon. And though she is gone, her absence fills every space, her memory etched in every moment. We did all we could, and yet, it never feels like it was enough.

Chapter 56: A Promise through the Years: Carrying Her Love Forward

It's been 25 years since that day—25 years since everything changed, leaving a mark on all of us that will never fully fade. Losing her brought our family closer, but it was a closeness forged in pain, a bond built on the heartache we all felt, each in our own way. My children felt it deeply, but none more so than my daughter, Shanna. To this day, she struggles to let go, to move past the sorrow that still lives in her heart. They say time heals, but in this case, the sadness has remained, touching each of us differently, yet binding us together in our grief.

For Shanna, though, that sadness is something she still carries with her, a weight that never really lifts. I only hope she knows that her mother is watching over her, over all her beautiful children and grandchildren, keeping them safe from a distance. I believe, with all my heart that she's there, protecting them, surrounding them with her love.

When she passed, it's strange, but certain memories remain so clear. I remember writing down my promise to her—a vow that I would protect our children with everything in me, that I would guide them through life with as much love as I could give, so they would know they are cherished, that they would have true happiness in their lives. It was a promise made in the depths of grief, yet one that has shaped every choice I've made since.

I hope, with all my heart, that I've kept that promise, that I haven't let her down. In the quiet moments, I feel her presence, a reminder of the love we shared and the family we built together. And I hold onto that, hoping she sees the life we've created and finds peace in knowing that, even in her absence, she is still here, still loved, still a part of everything we do.

Chapter 57: The Day Life Tested Me Beyond Measure

Not long after Jackie passed, just as we were beginning to face the immense void her absence left, life delivered another blow. My eldest son, Rudi, was diagnosed with schizophrenia. Deep down, I had known he wasn't well, even before Jackie's illness. She saw it too, but I had buried my head in the sand, unwilling to face it, hoping it would pass. But with Jackie gone, I could no longer ignore the reality in front of me.

Rudi had always been a beautiful soul, gentle and kind, but as Jackie grew sicker, he started to unravel. It was as though he, too, was slipping away, in a different, heart-breaking way. And suddenly, not long after losing my wife, I was facing this new, unimaginable struggle. I had five children to care for, and my eldest was fighting an invisible battle that was tearing him apart and tearing us apart. Eventually, it reached a point where he needed to be sectioned; he had become lost in his own mind, beyond anything I could help him with on my own.

It was as if the universe had decided to test every ounce of strength I had. I found myself grappling with the heartbreak of Jackie's passing, the daily responsibilities of raising our children, and now, the unimaginable task of supporting a son with mental illness. I felt like I was being pushed to the very edge, wondering why this was happening, why our family had been dealt such a difficult hand.

I had to make a decision—one that tore at my heart, one of the hardest decisions I've ever faced. I had to let Rudi go, place him in care, knowing he'd go from one home to another. I remember the anguish in each step of the process, the endless wrestling within me, hoping I could somehow find another way. Each month, he would come back to us for a few days, and those visits were bittersweet, filled with love but shadowed by the ache of knowing he couldn't stay. Even now, each time he returns, I ask myself if I made the right choice. And each time, I feel the same quiet sorrow, the weight of a decision I'll carry with me forever.

But I knew then, and I know now, that it was the only choice I could have made. If I hadn't let him go, he would have slowly, unintentionally, torn our lives apart.

It wasn't his fault—he couldn't see the toll his illness took on us, the way it strained us to our limits. And so, I bore that weight alone, the weight of knowing that my decision to keep our family safe would mean he couldn't be with us in the way we had once dreamed.

Rudi is now in his 40s, and while his life has taken a different path, he still has a family who loves him deeply. We see him every month, and whatever he needs, it's his without a moment's hesitation. No matter where he is, he knows he's not alone, that we are here for him, always.

In the quiet moments, I still feel the sadness, the heartbreak of what could never be. But I hold on to the hope that he understands, that he knows his family's love surrounds him. I made this choice for us all, but most of all, I made it with nothing but love for him in my heart. And though it broke me, it was a choice born of the deepest care for him and for the family we fought to hold together.

Chapter 58: A Heart-breaking Choice; The Sacrifice Only a Parent Could Make

As I look back on my life, one of the heaviest decisions I ever had to make was not allowing my son, Rudi, to live with us. I knew that if he stayed, his illness would gradually tear our family apart, yet no one truly understood the depth of that choice or the pain it caused me. I shouldered the burden alone, carrying the sadness and heartbreak of pushing my eldest son away to protect those he loved most.

My children never saw the silent pain that haunted me, the countless nights I lay awake, tears streaming down my face as I questioned myself. Had I failed him? Was there some other way, something I'd overlooked? They didn't feel the crushing weight of that decision, the way it lodged in my heart, and a constant ache that made me feel as though I'd let him down in the most fundamental way a parent can.

It was a responsibility that never left me, lingering in every quiet moment, pressing down on my shoulders, a burden I carried alone. This was not a choice made lightly or out of convenience. It was a choice born of love, a love that was so fierce it demanded I sacrifice my own comfort, my own peace, to protect them. I didn't make this decision for myself. I made it for all of them—for my family, for Rudi, and for the hope that they might find stability and happiness without the shadows of his illness pulling them down.

In my heart, I knew that if he stayed, the damage would be inevitable, unrelenting, and devastating. So I took on the pain of that choice, alone, hoping that one day they'd understand that my actions came from a place of love—a love so profound it meant stepping back, holding my grief inside, and doing what I believed would keep them safe.

Chapter 59: Embracing the Chaos; A Life Full of Laughter and Surprises

Life hasn't always been a story of struggle and heartache—there have been countless happy, absurd, and downright hilarious moments, and I'm truly grateful for every one of them. In fact, some of the funniest moments have come at the most unexpected times, right when I thought life couldn't possibly surprise me any more than it already had.

So now, it's time to dive into the lighter side, to take a look at the ridiculous misadventures, the twists of fate, and the laugh-out-loud moments that have kept me on my toes. That's what this book is really about: the strange, wild, and wonderfully unpredictable journey that is life—mine, and maybe even a bit of yours.

Because here's the thing: no matter how well you plan or how carefully you think you're steering the ship, life has a way of saying, "Not so fast!" You think you've got it figured out, but suddenly you're chasing a mouse around the kitchen, or trying to explain why there's a turkey loose in your living room (don't worry, we'll get to that one later).

So, if you're ready to join me on this rollercoaster of mishaps, laughs, and unexpected joy, then hold on tight. What could possibly go wrong? Well, my friend, you're about to find out

Chapter 60: What could possibly go wrong, right?

So here we go again—what could possibly go wrong, right? Well, let me set the scene. After my wife passed away, we decided it was time to move. It was just too painful to stay in the house, even though it held a lot of good memories. With five kids and no TV to distract us, you can imagine we were all feeling a little... tense.

The sale of the house went through smoothly enough, and we cleared everything out. We found a beautiful new house just around the corner. Now, everything seems to be going well, which, as you've probably gathered by now, is usually a red flag in my life.

There were still a few things in the loft that I needed to move out before the new owner, Darren, started gutting the place for a full makeover—extensions, rewiring, the works. So, naturally, I went up to the loft to grab those last few bits. Simple, right?

Spoiler alert: It's me. So, of course, things didn't stay simple for long.

Darren, the new owner, told me he'd give me a shout when he started the loft conversion—just in case I needed to grab anything I'd left behind before he transformed the space into his personal paradise. "Sure, no problem!" I said, thinking I'd left a few things, but nothing major.

Fast forward a few weeks, and the call comes in. Darren's ready to tear into the loft, and suddenly it hits me: I might have left a bit more up there than I remembered. No big deal, though, right? I'll just pop over and grab it all real quick.

Now, if you've been following along, you know with me, nothing is ever "real quick."

It's the middle of winter, the house is fully renovated except for the loft, and Darren had thoughtfully left the front door open and a ladder leading to the loft. No lights downstairs, of course, but hey, there's a single bulb in the loft. That should do the trick, right? So, I climb the ladder into the pitch-black abyss, flick the light on, and there it is: the attic version of a hoarder's paradise. Boxes stacked like Tetris blocks, dust thicker than fog, and all sorts of forgotten treasures from years gone by.

Halfway through the treasure hunt, I notice something weird stuck to a beam—a beam, mind you, that's basically the only thing keeping me from falling through the unboarded floor and into the freshly renovated house below. "What's that?" I think to myself, because, you know, I'm nosy by nature.

Now, you'd think common sense would kick in, but no, not me. I grab a stick, and like a curious idiot, I start poking at this mysterious thing stuck to the beam. As I prod it, something becomes painfully clear: it's a wasp nest.

Next thing I know, I'm in the middle of a wasp apocalypse, getting swarmed like I just declared war on the entire wasp population. My panic mode kicks in, and I make a mad dash for the ladder, except... remember that beam? Yeah, I miss it completely. One second I'm running for my life, the next I'm free-falling through the ceiling like some kind of poorly executed magic trick.

I open my eyes, and there it is—a giant hole in the ceiling where, just moments before, a beautiful chandelier had been. Now? The chandelier is in pieces, shattered all over the floor, and I'm lying there, covered in plaster, dust, and pure humiliation. To top it off, there are still angry wasps buzzing around like they're out for revenge. Again? I thought. This cannot be happening again.

I somehow manage to hobble out, probably looking like I'd just survived a natural disaster, and make it home. That's when I realise I've got to call Darren and explain this little situation.

"Hey, Darren. Good news and bad news. The good news? You can just throw everything in the loft away. The bad news? I fell through the ceiling, demolished your chandelier, and there's a bloody big hole in the ceiling... well, let's just say it's going to need a little TLC."

There's a pause. Then Darren, with a laugh that only a saint or a madman could muster, says, "No worries, mate. I'll sort it out. What could possibly go wrong, eh?"

I had to agree. That was a stupid question.

Now, here's the thing—I never told Darren about the wasp nest. Do you think I should have? Nooooo. Some things are better left unsaid. He's already dealing with a giant hole in his ceiling and a shattered chandelier; the last thing he needs is to know about the wasp army I unleashed in his attic. Let him think it was just gravity that got the better of me, not my nosy stick-poking at a wasp mansion.

Ignorance is bliss, right?

Chapter 61: A Journey through Life's Challenges

As time went on, life became a whirlwind. I bounced from one job to another, chasing opportunities, dodging disasters, and somehow keeping it all together. But life had a way of throwing curveballs, and the biggest one of all was losing Jackie. Bless her, she was my rock, the one who kept me grounded through every madcap scheme and every leap of faith.

Suddenly, I found myself bringing up five kids on my own. Five! Talk about stepping into uncharted territory. Every day felt like I was juggling flaming swords while riding a unicycle. School runs, packed lunches, endless laundry—it was like running a full-time operation, only without the manual.

But as chaotic as it was, those kids became my driving force. They gave me a reason to keep going, to find the next job, to face the next challenge. Every time I wanted to throw in the towel, I'd look at them and think, Nope. Can't let them down.

Jackie may have passed, but her influence never left. I'd hear her voice in my head during the toughest moments, telling me to keep going, to make it work. And somehow, through all the madness, I did.

I remember the day like it was yesterday. I came home after another soul-crushing day working for British Gas, knocking on doors in the freezing cold, the middle of winter biting through to my bones. That day, I'd had enough. I was done with the endless grind, the knock-backs, and the relentless monotony of it all. It was the day I realised something big: I needed to stop chasing jobs I hated and start doing what I'd been doing a good part of my life without even realising it.

It had been staring me in the face the whole time—hypnosis. I'd been practising it wholeheartedly for years, but never once thought it could be the thing to turn my life around. It took my boys, Josh and Zak, to open my eyes. One day, while I was out, they cleared out a whole room in the house. Furniture gone, space ready. When I walked in, I thought, "What the hell's going on here?"

Before I could say a word, they looked at me and said, "Do what you love, Dad. Hypnosis."

I couldn't believe it. They thought I'd be angry, but I wasn't. In fact, I was stunned. They saw what I couldn't—what had been right there in front of me all along. They'd given me a nudge, and suddenly, it all made sense.

I'd been trained by my uncle, a stage hypnotist, back in the day. Over time, I'd become a hypnoanalyst, helping people get to the root of their issues. It was something I was passionate about, something I was good at. And now, for the first time, I realised I could make it my life's work.

It's funny, isn't it? Sometimes, you need a wake-up call—or in my case, a cleared-out room and two determined sons—to see what's been right in front of you all along. That was the day I decided to take the leap, to take a risk on myself and do what I loved. And from that moment, everything started to change.

Well, from that turning point, life took me on a journey I could have never imagined. I travelled all over the world, learning everything I could about the mind, hypnosis, and psychology. I soaked it all up like a sponge, hungry for knowledge, determined to master the craft that had been quietly calling to me my entire life.

And you know what? Life did change—for the better. I became the best at what I did. The money started coming in, but more importantly, I found my purpose. I became the author of seven books; the creator of Inherited Therapy and founder of the Loveday Method—a technique that changed the lives of so many people. To this day, I'm still writing, still learning, and, most importantly, still helping others.

Through it all, I learned the most valuable lesson of all: when you work with someone, it's not about their mind—it's about their heart. That's where true transformation happens. The mind might resist, but the heart? That's where the real healing begins.

Looking back, every challenge, every risk, and every "what could possibly go wrong" moment led me to this. To do what I love, what I'm good at, and what I was meant to do. And for that, I'm endlessly grateful.

I've come to realise that life is a circle—constantly turning, bringing us back to lessons we need to learn. We all have our strengths and weaknesses, and the journey isn't about avoiding them but understanding and embracing them.

For me, that circle brought me back to what I was always meant to do: helping others, not just through the mind but through the heart. I found my strengths in connecting with people, in understanding their struggles, and guiding them toward healing and transformation. And my weaknesses? Well, they taught me resilience, humility, and the value of never giving up.

In the end, that's the beauty of life. It's not about perfection—it's about growth. And in finding my strengths, I found my purpose.

Chapter 62: The Three-Piece Suite Disaster: My Joyride from Hell

What could possibly go wrong? Well, hang tight, because you're about to find out. So, I'm working for my brother again. You'd think he'd have more sense after all the damage I've caused over the years, but here we are. The usual driver was off sick, and he needed me to fill in. "Just drive the van," he said, with a very firm warning to not go inside the customer's home. Apparently, he hadn't forgotten the time I nearly demolished a house by putting a wardrobe through the ceiling and smashing a chandelier. But, hey, desperate times.

It's a beautiful summer day, and we're headed to Wales to pick up a three-piece-suite to be reupholstered. Easy enough, right? Just drive the van, with two guys to do the heavy lifting. What could go wrong? Famous last words.

To my surprise, we found the house easily, tucked away in the Welsh countryside, with lots of steep hills and some particularly high speed bumps. But the guys load the suite into the van in no time, and we're back on the road.

Now, I'd mentioned those hills and speed bumps, right? Well, we're driving back, and there's this especially high speed bump coming up. We go over it, and the next thing I hear is this almighty bang from the back of the van. The whole vehicle feels like it's gone airborne for a second, and then—silence. No rumble from the engine, just pure, eerie silence.

I glance in the rear-view mirror, and there's this giant metal thing lying in the middle of the road behind us. Then it hits me: the brakes are gone. Completely gone. And we're barrelling down this steep hill, picking up speed like we're auditioning for the next Fast & Furious.

The lads in the back are blissfully unaware, while I'm gripping the wheel, white-knuckled, realising that we're basically in a runaway van on a joyride to doom. If I survive this, I'm definitely renegotiating my pay… assuming my brother doesn't fire me on the spot.

Well, we did stop... by slamming into a huge lamppost! And when I say "stop," I mean we reduced that poor lamppost to a pile of scrap. There's barely anything left of it—or the van, for that matter. The guys in the back are wide-eyed, looking like they've just seen a ghost. And I'm sitting there, dazed, wondering why the brakes just gave up on us.

Then, as if things couldn't get worse, the bonnet pops open. I take a peek and say to the lads, "Uh... is the engine supposed to be in front of the van?" They give me this look, as if I'm asking whether water's supposed to be wet, and one of them goes, "Well, yeah, obviously."

So I reply, "Then where the bloody hell is it?!"

And that's when it hits me, like a brick to the face—that massive hunk of metal we left in the road three miles back? Yep, that was the engine. It had popped right out when we went over the speed bump. We've been coasting down the hill in a van without an engine.

I'm sitting there, feeling the weight of impending doom settle in. All I can think is, "Oh my god, my brother's going to kill me." I mean, I've messed up before, but leaving the engine three miles behind us? I've outdone myself this time!

You know, my brother Morris didn't have a single grey hair until I started working for him. At this rate, he's going to be bald by next week when he finds out what happened today. I mean, how the heck are we even getting home? And how am I going to break the news to him?

We spot a phone box—no mobiles back then—so I shove some coins in and dial his number, already bracing myself. He answers with a heavy sigh, like he's pre-emptively disappointed. "You're not going to believe this," I start.

There's a pause, then: "What have you done now, Geoffrey?"

My heart's pounding, and I'm thinking, "Okay, keep it cool." So, he asked, "Have you caused any damage to the house?

The house is fine,

Have you damaged the furniture?

"Of course not," I assure him. I can almost feel the relief on the other end of the line. "Thank god for that," he says. "Then what is it?"

I take a deep breath. "Well... we're going to need a tow truck. I, uh, smashed up your van."

Then silence. I could almost see his face turning beet red through the phone. "It's not my bloody van, Geoffrey! It's a rental!"

"Oh, brilliant. Well, you better tell the rental company that van's a death trap! Trust me." Let's just say... that didn't go over well.

I tried to lighten the mood and said, "Well, I hope you got insurance, you know... the one that covers complete disasters?"

There's this heavy pause, then he grumbles, "Not that insurance, Geoffrey. The basic one."

"Oh, so not the 'Total Write-Off' package?" I ask, trying to keep a straight face.

He is absolutely losing it on the other end. I could almost feel the vein popping in his forehead as he groaned, "Geoffrey, you are literally the reason that package exists!"

Honestly, if I survive this conversation, I deserve a medal... or at least my own insurance plan—one that covers "Geoffrey-level" catastrophes.

"Bloody good job you're in the RAC,

" he replied

I'm not in the RAC."

There was a silence so heavy you could feel it. Then I roared, "You're NOT in the bloody RAC?!

How exactly are you planning to get me home, then? PUSH the thing back?!"

I can practically hear him pinching the bridge of his nose in utter frustration, probably wishing for some kind of "Geoffrey Eraser" button.

"Where are you?" he grumbled, barely holding it together.

I gave him my location, hoping for some sympathy, but instead, he just let out this weary sigh. "Right. I'll sort a tow truck. And when you're back, don't even think about slinking off anywhere—I want you in my office. Don't make any plans tonight, Geoffrey. I want to hear every excruciating detail about how you managed to cause this mess."

Now, this is where I try my best to defend myself. "Look, I know it sounds bad, but honestly, this time it really wasn't my fault."

There's this deadly pause, and then he lets out a sarcastic snort. "Oh, brilliant. Not your fault, is it, Geoffrey? How convenient."

His voice drips with sarcasm. "Go on, then—enlighten me. Was it the van's fault? The weather's fault? Or did a mysterious ghost shove your foot down on the pedal?"

I scramble to come up with an excuse that sounds halfway believable. "I wouldn't mind," I say, grasping for sympathy, "but, really, it isn't!"

He let out a sigh so deep it probably shook the rental company's phone lines. "Geoffrey, you know what? I'm at the point where I'd believe anything with you. Let's just get you back, and I'll bring my blood pressure tablets to the office meeting."

By now, I'm sweating bullets, wondering if I'll even make it through the night. And in the back of my mind, I'm thinking, Next time, I'll take the bloody bus.

So, I finally arrived back at the office, bracing myself for the interrogation. I walk in, and my brother Morris is already glaring at me like I just set fire to his favourite suit.

I take a deep breath, hoping maybe—maybe—he'll understand. "Listen, Morris," I start, "it wasn't my fault. I hit this bump in the road, right? And then, out of nowhere, the engine practically drops out of the van. We're barrelling down a mountain road at 80 miles an hour, no brakes—no brakes, Morris! Honestly, we're lucky to be alive."

Does he sympathise? Not in the slightest. He doesn't say, "Oh, Geoffrey, you're more important than the van." Nope. Instead, his face turns red, and he starts muttering words I'm pretty sure were banned in half the world's languages. The man's hitting notes only dogs can hear, absolutely fuming.

Then he narrows his eyes at me, like he's got me all figured out. "So let me get this straight," he says slowly, voice dripping with sarcasm.

"What you're telling me is that you just sheared the bolts off, wrecked the van, and then took it for a little joyride down a mountain… with no brakes… all because it sounded like a good time?"

I'm trying to keep a straight face, but my defence is going down faster than that van. "Are you serious, Morris? You think I thought, 'Hey, wouldn't it be a blast to test my survival skills with a death-ride down a mountain road?'"

But he's not letting me off that easily. He points a finger at me, practically shaking with exasperation.

"Geoffrey, you are single-handedly propping up the entire tow truck industry! At this rate, I'm going to need to hire someone to follow you around full-time with a toolbox and a roll of duct tape!"

By this point, I realise there's no escape. He's practically ready to ground me—yes, as a grown man—for life. And just as I'm hoping he might be finished, he leans in one last time, dripping with sarcasm.

"Next time, Geoffrey, try something new. Maybe drive on a flat, paved road, at a normal speed, and, if it's not too much to ask, with brakes that work."

So, the rental company gets involved, the insurance guy shows up, pokes around the wreckage, and after a long sigh, tells me, "This van shouldn't have been on the road in the first place. You're lucky to be alive." Finally, someone is on my side! It is officially not my fault.

Now, did I get an apology from Morris? Of course not! He just gives me that classic "Geoffrey-is-the-bane-of-my-existence" look and grumbles under his breath. But I wasn't about to let him off that easily.

So, later that night, when things have just barely calmed down, I decide to casually ask, "By the way, boss, when can I expect my wages for today?"

I swear, you could actually see his blood pressure going up in real-time. His face turned shades of red, like a kettle about to explode. If I hadn't known better, I'd have checked for steam coming out of his ears. Poor guy probably aged five years on the spot!

I swear, if I make it out of this alive, I'm buying him a year's supply of blood pressure tablets.

Chapter 63: The Great Car Heist Fiasco: What Else Could Possibly Go Wrong?

So, the XR41 gets stolen right out of the driveway. And here's the thing—there wasn't a drop of petrol in it. Whoever nabbed it probably got half a mile down the road before realising they'd just stolen themselves a glorified garden ornament.

I imagine the thief sitting there, banging the wheel, realising their "great escape" would be a "great walk home" instead. Probably the first carjacking in history where the getaway car needed rescuing more than they did!

So, that's exactly what happened. I got home late from an appointment, barely made it back because the fuel gauge was practically coughing on fumes. Figured I'd deal with it in the morning.

Next day, I get up, grab the keys, head out to take the kids to school, look at the driveway... and there's just an empty patch of pavement staring back at me. My beautiful car—gone! Stolen!

I dash back into the house, shouting to Jackie, "The car's been nicked! I'm calling the police!" As I'm dialling, though, this horrible thought hits me—wasn't the insurance due yesterday? My stomach sinks. Great. Not only is the car gone, but I'm pretty sure I'm not insured either.

The police finally answer, and I explain the whole situation, adding, "And, uh, just so you know, I think my insurance ran out yesterday."

There's a pause, and then the officer actually starts laughing! Like this was the best news he'd heard all day. Meanwhile, I'm standing there with the phone, thinking, "Are you kidding me? Absolute waste of time!"

I hang up, turn to Jackie, and shake my head. "Well, the car's officially vanished, the police think I'm a contestant on Britain's Got Talent, and the insurance company? They're probably holding a company-wide laugh session at my expense.

Guess I'll walk the kids to school

So, I'm standing there thinking, "What else could possibly go wrong?" when I realise Jackie's Mini is parked out on the road. Perfect! I'll just take the kids in that. So, I pile everyone out the door, and just as we're about to get into the Mini, I glance down the street and—hang on. There's my car! Sitting a bit crooked, all doors open, lights flashing on and off like it's doing some kind of SOS signal.

I hustle the kids back inside, thinking, "What kind of thief returns a stolen car?" I head down to investigate and, sure enough, the car's there, but it's a total wreck.

They've ripped out half the wiring in some attempt to hotwire it... but here's the best part: they must've run out of fuel halfway through the theft.

So they're stuck, in the car, trying everything to get it started, but it's going absolutely nowhere! Can you imagine their faces? They've just stolen themselves a two-ton paperweight.

So there we are, pushing the car like it's some kind of tank, trying to get it back onto the driveway. It took three of us and half the neighbourhood watching, trying not to laugh.

Finally, we got it back, called in an auto electrician to fix the mess, and once it was running again, we sold it. Never looked back!

Honestly, the whole thing just goes to show... what else could possibly go wrong?

Well you are about to find out.

Chapter 64: Why Do These Things Always Happen to Me?

You'd think it couldn't happen again, right? Wrong. It always happens to me. So, there I am, driving down the road in a massive Luton van, minding my own business, when suddenly, a wheel rolls right past us. I think, "Huh, some poor soul's lost a wheel." And then it hits me—that bloody wheel is from the van I'm driving.

Yep. My van has shed a wheel, mid-drive, like it's throwing a tantrum. And guess who I'm working for again? My brother, Morris. The same guy who still hasn't forgiven me for the "engine-fell-out" incident. To this day, he thinks I somehow planned that disaster.

Now, this van's got four wheels on the back, so technically we're still rolling, but I know Morris is going to lose it when he finds out. The man already believes I have some kind of mechanical curse. I'm convinced he thinks I bribed the insurance adjuster last time just to avoid the blame!

When I call to break the news, I can practically hear the vein in his forehead popping. I'm half expecting him to scream, "Geoffrey, are you actively trying to dismantle every vehicle I own, piece by piece?" Honestly, after this, I wouldn't be surprised if he issues a company-wide memo: Effective immediately, Geoffrey is banned from all machinery with wheels, engines, or moving parts.

"I Swear, the Universe is having the Last Laugh... at MY expense! From runaway wheels to falling engines, I've seen it all!"

It's like the universe has me on speed dial for slapstick disasters. Every time I think, "It can't possibly happen again", I find myself chasing after a runaway wheel, or explaining to my brother why his van's engine is now sitting in pieces. From insurance mishaps to police calls that sound like stand-up comedy routines, it's as if every vehicle I touch has a countdown clock for catastrophe.

Honestly, I'm convinced some cosmic prankster is watching, popcorn in hand, just waiting for my next move!

Chapter 65: How Tight Jeans Nearly Ruined My Life

Trust me, this was the least funny thing to happen at five in the morning getting ready for work. Picture it: I'm half-awake, barely functioning, and trying to squeeze myself into my tightest jeans—because why not make life harder before coffee, right? So I hike them up, go for the zip, and then... disaster. The zip catches, and not just on the fabric. Oh, no. This is skin-in-the-zip kind of caught, the kind of pain that shoots through you and makes you question all of your life choices.

Now, I'm standing on the bed, frozen in place, realising the predicament I'm in. It's still pitch dark, and Jackie's fast asleep next to me, blissfully unaware of my personal horror movie unfolding a foot away. I'm whispering, desperately, "Jackie! Jackie!" like a ghost haunting the bedroom, hoping she'll wake up and rescue me. All I get is a grumpy groan, "Let me sleep, let me sleep!"

Meanwhile, I'm sweating bullets, balancing like a flamingo on the edge of the bed, my life flashing before my eyes. The pain is unreal. I'm starting to think, "This is it. I've ended my sex life... all because of a cheap zipper."

And there's this horrible moment where I realise: I've only got two options. Option one: wake the whole neighbourhood with a bloodcurdling scream. Option two: go in, grit my teeth, and try to get free without losing anything I might need later. So there I am, wrestling with the jeans like I'm in a death match, practically performing acrobatics that should be in the Olympics, whisper-screaming like some madman on the edge.

After what feels like an eternity of silent agony, contortions, and soul-searching, I finally—finally—get loose. I'm drenched in sweat, I'm exhausted, and I swear I could hear the universe laughing at me. Those jeans? Straight to the bin. The trauma? That's going to stick with me for life.

And let's just say, from that day forward, I made a solemn vow: loose pants only.

Chapter 66: Hooked on Trouble: How I Keep Falling for Zak's 'Brilliant' Ideas

Alright, here we go. So Zak, at the grand age of eight, already fancies himself a business prodigy. He's clever with numbers, a whiz with gadgets, so naturally, I think a little tech device will keep him occupied, maybe teach him a thing or two. Little did I know, it would spark the entrepreneurial scheme of the century.

One day, he comes up to me, eyes bright, and says, "I've got a great idea! Why don't we sell phones?" And like an absolute bloody lunatic, I think, "Yeah, why not?" He's got that confidence, you know? He looks like he knows what he's talking about—how bad could it be?

So, Zak's plan: we'll sell phones on eBay. But instead of spending our own money, we'll use the customers' money through PayPal, buy the phones directly from suppliers in China, and ship them straight to the buyers. No upfront costs, no inventory, just pure profit. It's fool proof, right? And remember, this is coming from an eight-year-old.

That's right—an eight-year-old is standing there, pitching me this grand scheme with all the confidence of a Silicon Valley CEO, and there I am, like a bloody idiot, not just listening but cheering him on! I'm standing there, nodding along, saying, "Zak, that's a brilliant idea!" like he's just unlocked the secrets of the stock market. The kid's still learning his times tables, and here I am, mentally drafting up business cards and planning our corporate logo. Honestly, he says, "Let's sell phones," and suddenly I'm thinking, "Why stop there? Let's build an empire!

So, off we go, listing these phones at £500 to £800 each, with our big "profits" being around £50 to £80 per sale. And guess what? In just the first week, we raked in £40,000. Forty grand! I'm thinking this kid's a prodigy. Richard Branson who? I'm already planning our next venture in my head.

Then—bam. The reality check. Turns out, every single one of these bloody stupid phones is a complete fake. I'm talking about phones that wouldn't pass as a prop on a bad TV show. Customers are furious, eBay blacklists us, PayPal hits us with an eye-watering £1,800 in debt, and suddenly, I'm faced with the charming task of contacting every single customer to beg for forgiveness and pay back every penny.

So there I am, tallying up the disaster, and it dawns on me just how much this "brilliant idea" has cost me. I turn to Zak, the mastermind behind it all, and say, "Do you have any idea how much you've just cost me?"

He looks at me, totally unfazed, gives a little shrug, and says, "Why on earth would you listen to an eight-year-old?"

He's right why would I listen to an eight year old;

Honestly, lesson learned: never trust a kid with a business idea that sounds too good to be true—or a business idea at all, for that matter! I'll tell you one thing, though. Next time he comes up with "a great idea," I'm locking my wallet and running the other way!

Now, you'd think after that fiasco, I'd bolt at the very mention of Zak's next "big idea," right? But, of course not. Somehow, he'd reel me right back in, every single time! It's like the universe had front-row seats to our misadventures and kept nudging me, "Go on, trust him again—what could possibly go wrong?"

Honestly, I'm pretty sure it was karma. Zak would get that glint in his eye, hit me with, "Dad, I've got another great idea," and before I knew it, I'd be nodding along, thinking, "What harm could it do this time? Famous last words.

It's like I'd developed some bizarre, self-destructive reflex. Every time he pitched a new scheme, I'd just lean in closer, like, "Tell me more, my young prodigy." And each time, I'd end up with less cash, more headaches, and a growing suspicion that my bank account and blood pressure were in a pact to finish me off.

So, yes, in hindsight, maybe I should've run. But let's be real—I didn't stand a chance against Zak's "business brain."

Here's the real twist—what I didn't see coming was that this little eight-year-old, with his over-the-top ideas and wild schemes, would actually go on to build a multi-million-pound business as he got older. Yep, the same kid who convinced me to dive into that phone-selling disaster grew up to be a serious business powerhouse. Turns out, all those "brilliant ideas" were just the beginning!

Would you believe that Zak actually thinks he made me money? Zak genuinely believes he was some sort of financial wizard, like he single-handedly built me a fortune with his "brilliant" ideas! Meanwhile, I'm here counting the losses and grey hairs, thinking,

If only you knew.

Chapter 67: Trust Me, It Wasn't Just Zak—Then Came Josh, and Together They Became the Double Trouble Duo!

If you thought one kid with "genius ideas" was bad, let me introduce you to Zak and Josh, my very own dynamic duo of double trouble. With Zak's clever schemes and Josh's eager backup, it was like having my own pair of mini masterminds conspiring daily to pull me into the next big fiasco. Just when I thought I might be safe from Zak's plans, in swoops Josh with a grin, ready to help make the next wild idea even bigger. Together? They're unstoppable—costing me time, cash, and what's left of my sanity!

Let me tell you about Josh and Zak, the twin brothers of mayhem. They've been in double trouble since diaper days, and yours truly—yes, me—has been their favourite partner in crime (unwillingly drafted, of course). You'd think two heads are better than one, but in their case, it's just double the mischief.

As kids, they had more plots than a graveyard, and guess who the star was always? Me, with my wallet wide open. My blood pressure was like a rollercoaster designed by a mad scientist, and my bank account? Let's just say it saw more exits than entrances.

Let me tell you about Josh, my very own agent of chaos. When we were younger, Josh had more schemes than a soap opera villain. Of course, I always ended up roping in, wallet first. My blood pressure was like a yo-yo and my bank account looked like it was on a diet. As we got older, Josh's ideas only got bigger. One day, he came to me with his biggest pitch yet: "Let's invest in digital products!" Before I knew it, I'd forked over £12,000. The big thing? We couldn't sell the bloody things.

Believe it or not, I'm pretty sure my hair started falling because of it. What can I say? Who needs enemies when you've got entrepreneurial sons like Josh and Zak?

Chapter 68: The Ruby Ring: A Precious Memory Passed Down

This is one of those days you never forget—a day that leaves you smiling, mixed with wonder and a bit of magic. When Jackie passed, I wanted to keep her memory alive in a way that felt real, so I decided to give her ruby ring to our eldest daughter. She was about sixteen at the time, and when I handed it to her, the look on her face said everything; it was as though she'd been given the world. From then on, she wore it every day, keeping a little piece of Jackie close to her heart.

That ring wasn't just jewellery; it was memories and love wrapped up in a perfect, simple circle. It was Jackie's laughter, her warmth, her spirit, and you could tell it gave Shanna a kind of quiet connection—something timeless and deeply special. Even now, just thinking of that ring brings back a flood of happy memories—the joy Jackie brought into our lives.

But two years later, when Shanna was about eighteen, she came home one day, tears streaming down her face. She'd lost her mum's ring—the one that made her feel so close to Jackie. Her heartbreak was written all over her, and we spent hours searching everywhere, turning the house upside down, but it was gone. It was devastating. The ring had been part of her daily life, and now, suddenly, it wasn't.

Fast-forward 26 years to COVID, when we had all that rare time on our hands. The weather was perfect, and I decided it was finally time to clear out the garage—a massive, double garage packed to the brim with years of forgotten odds and ends. Little did I know, that day would bring so much more than just a good clear-out.

As I dug through layers of boxes, I noticed an old Quicksave bag buried beneath a pile. Curious, I opened it up and found Shanna's university diary, a little worn and dusty. And then, as I lifted the diary, something shiny caught my eye—a glint of red, hidden in the corner of the bag. I stopped, blinked, looked closer, and couldn't believe it. It was Jackie's ruby ring.

My hands were shaking as I took it out of the bag, barely able to breathe, half convinced it was a dream. I had to see it for myself, compare it, and know it was real.

I took a picture of the ring, then found an old photo of Jackie wearing it and sent both to Shanna. When she called, she was in tears, just as overwhelmed and filled with joy as I was.

You see, that ring had been lost for 26 long years. What are the odds of finding it again after all that time? It felt like a miracle, one of those moments you simply can't explain. But I'll always be convinced Jackie had a hand in it, guiding me right to that old Quicksave bag on that beautiful, sunny day, making sure the ring found its way back to us. It's like she was saying, "I'm still here with you."

Chapter 69: The Secret Commando Wound: How a 10-Year-Old Cowboy Healed Himself

This was one of those classic "what could possibly go wrong?" moments. We'd just moved to Gateacre Park Drive, I was about 10, and let me tell you, I loved that house. It was a place full of laughter, surprises, and yeah, some chaos too, but those memories are priceless. It was a summer day, one of those unbelievably sunny ones you only got back then, and, of course, I was up to no good as usual. Honestly, I'm convinced to this day I'm not from this planet.

So, there I am, looking for some excitement. Bentley, my brother, had made it very clear—under "threat of death," mind you—that I was never to go into his room. But let's be real. This is me we're talking about—no fear, no rules.

Naturally, I sneak in, look around, and what do I find under his bed? An enormous Bowie knife, sheathed, with an eight-inch blade that was like a mini sword to a 10-year-old. I'm awestruck. Back then, laws were different, and apparently, so was common sense, because my first thought was, "What a find!"

So, I strap the knife to a belt, feeling like an absolute commando. I even go the extra mile and put black stripes on my face—don't ask me what I used; all I know is I looked like a highly-trained, highly-dangerous… 10-year-old. I'm all geared up, heart racing, thinking, "What harm could this do?"

Adventure mode activated, I head outside. The countryside was practically our backyard, so off I go, running, jumping, diving through fields like I'm on some secret mission. I've got the knife in hand, making action-movie rolls left and right, having the time of my life.

Until I slip. Next thing I know, I'm on the ground, staring at a one-inch gash in my leg. Blood is everywhere, and I can see all the way to the bone, with a sinew sticking out like a bit of spaghetti that refused to stay inside.

At this point, the commando act is long gone. I limp home, blood pouring down my leg, and all I can think is, "My dad is going to kill me!" If I don't bleed out first, I'm going to be dead the second he walks through the door. And as for Bentley? Well, I don't even want to think about what he's going to do when he sees his precious knife covered in my blood.

Let's just say, that was the end of my commando career—and my last raid on Bentley's room!

Well maybe not.

This was sixty-one years ago, and let me tell you, I wouldn't advise anyone to try this! Honestly, it was a miracle I made it out in one piece. If you're ever tempted to play commando with a giant knife as a kid, just... don't. Trust me, it doesn't end well!

Well, I know I've done my fair share of stupid things, but hey, accidents happen. Anyway, back to the story.

Do I tell anyone about my little "adventure"? Of course not! I'd have been in massive trouble! (Kids, take note—you should always tell an adult when something like this happens. They actually know what to do, unlike ten-year-old me.)

But in my head, I'm still in full cowboy mode. So, like I'd seen in every Western ever, I grab a hankie—yep, we all had handkerchiefs back then—and tie it around my leg as a makeshift bandage really, really tight. And what do you know? Eventually, the bleeding stops, the wound closes up, and my leg heals. No one ever knew about my little mishap.

Was it my proudest moment? Probably not. But hey, it was an experience, and that's got to count for something, right?

Chapter 70: My holiday from hell

Wow, this is one of those stories everyone finds hilarious—everyone except me, that is. I was about 17, working at Henderson's, training to be a buyer, and somehow, I ended up on a holiday to Lloret de Mar in Spain with six lads from Kirkby in Liverpool. A real "what could go wrong?" kind of trip.

So we check into the hotel, and by day two, we're in the room, trying to figure out the plan for the night. Our room was on the first floor, overlooking the pool, which was about to be more important than I realised. Anyway, out of nowhere, the guys decide it'd be a brilliant idea to throw me into the pool—yes, from the balcony.

Now, if you've seen that James Bond scene where they throw the girl off the balcony into the pool and Bond says, "Lucky there was a pool there," that was me. Only difference was, I didn't feel lucky. Six guys lift me up like a rag doll, and the more I struggle, the worse it gets. Suddenly, I'm airborne, fully clothed, arms flailing, flying like a screaming Superman—straight toward the pool. I swear, I thought I was about to die.

Next thing I know, I smack into the water, clothes and all. And when I say fully clothed, I mean shoes, belts, everything. I climb out, looking like a drowned cat, dripping from head to toe, and head straight through the hotel reception, leaving a soggy trail behind me. The manager saw the whole thing—his expression was priceless, but trust me, he was not impressed. Neither was I, for that matter.

Meanwhile, the lads are hanging off the balcony, doubled over in hysterics, absolutely loving it. To this day, I don't know if they actually knew there was a pool below to save me or if they just lost their grip. All I know is, bloody hell, I could've died. But here's the kicker: that wasn't the end of it.

We were there for 14 nights, and trust me, those guys didn't just throw me into the pool once. Nope, this became the nightly entertainment. Ten times, they chucked me over that first-floor balcony into the pool like I was some kind of flying fish, each time with the same "hope-he-survives" drop that shaved a few years off my life.

And as if that wasn't enough, the hotel manager, who at first looked like he wanted to call the police, eventually started finding it funny too. Word spread fast, and soon, it wasn't just my so-called "mates" getting a laugh. The whole hotel got in on the act! By night four, I had a full-blown audience of holiday-goers camped out to watch "The Great Balcony Toss."

So there I was, every night, my own little death-defying act, fully clothed, flying into the pool to thunderous applause. People started to believe I was part of the evening entertainment, like I was on the hotel's payroll! Every time I dragged myself out of the water and walked, soaked and dripping, through the lobby, they'd all be waiting, 100 strong, cheering like they'd just watched a Broadway show. I half-expected someone to start handing out autographs.

In the end, I'd become the unofficial "pool act" of the hotel, and my friends? Well, they just doubled over in laughter, thrilled to have me as the hotel's nightly "show." And me? I'm still convinced I lost a year off my life every time I sailed over that balcony, but at least I got a fan club

But did it end there? Of course not. This was the holiday to remember—or in my case, the holiday to forget! Apparently, my so-called friends had a few more "genius" ideas lined up, just waiting to make my life flash before my eyes.

So what's next, you ask? Well, I'll tell you. After my nightly near-death experience of being flung off a balcony into the pool, you'd think I'd earned a bit of peace, right? Wrong. We end up going to a bullring. You know, a proper bullfight. Now, don't get me wrong, everyone should see a bullfight once, but what goes on there? It's terrifying! And I can personally vouch for that—because these lunatics, my "friends," get it into their heads that it would be hilarious to throw me into the ring with a live bull.

So there I am, chucked over the edge, landing smack in the middle of the bullring, and my "mates" are watching, doubled over, waiting to see what happens next. I'm thinking, "What happens?!" I'll tell you what bloody happens—I'm about to be squashed by half a ton of angry beef!

I freeze, literally rooted to the spot, and all I hear are people screaming, "¡Vamoose! ¡Vamoose!" which, as I quickly learned, means "Run like bloody hell!" But I'm frozen stiff because, you guessed it, I'm standing right next to this massive bull, staring down the business end of its horns, thinking "This is it. This is where it ends."

And as the bull starts snorting and pawing the ground, I realise my only option is to pull a full-speed sprint to the nearest exit. I take off like I'm training for the Olympics, heart pounding, legs pumping, with the bull hot on my heels, and my so-called friends hooting and cheering from the stands like they've paid good money for this live entertainment.

So there I am, face to face with this bull, when suddenly it charges. And I mean charges. I swear, it was inches away, its horns practically tickling my ribs. I don't know if it was adrenaline or sheer panic, but somehow, I managed to do a full somersault out of its path. One second I'm frozen in terror, the next, I'm flipping through the air like some kind of circus acrobat, dodging a bull that's bearing down on me like a freight train.

I hit the ground, barely believing I'm still alive, turn on my heel, and sprint back to the gate before the bull can even process what just happened. And thank God—someone had opened the doors. I burst through, panting, feeling every nerve in my body on fire, and what do I hear? Cheers. Actual cheering.

People are clapping, whistling, throwing flowers at me as if I've just given the performance of a lifetime! Flowers! I've barely survived the most terrifying experience of my life, thinking I'm about to end up as that bull's afternoon snack, and these people are acting like I'm the bloody matador!

Meanwhile, my so-called friends are laughing so hard they're practically rolling in the aisles. And me? I'm just trying to remember how to breathe, thinking, I almost died, and they're tossing roses.

Let me tell you, if there was ever a day to rethink my friendship choices, this was it!

Oh, you think it ended there? Are you kidding me? I'm with six absolute lunatics, and it's like the universe is sitting back with popcorn, loving every second of it. Meanwhile, all I want to do is go home, maybe curl up in a corner and cry. No one would believe half of what's happened on this holiday, but hey, we're in the last few days, and I've survived this so far. No more bullrings, no more balcony dives—what could possibly go wrong now, right?

So, that night, we decided to hit up a club called Explosion. It's 3 a.m., and we stumble out, singing and dancing in the street, completely carefree. Suddenly, this policeman walks up to one of the guys and smacks him right across the face! I'm thinking the policeman is speaking in Spanish.

We have no idea what he's saying, probably be quiet. I'm thinking, this isn't good. And what does my friend do? He steps right up to the policeman, looking like he's about to start round two. I'm practically frozen, thinking, "This is it. We're about to be arrested, or worse."

Next thing I know, the officer whips out a gun—and points it directly at me, yes me I haven't done anything. Within seconds, we're surrounded by half a dozen officers, all with their guns drawn, aimed squarely at us. And my friends? They're from Kirkby in Liverpool—they don't back down for anything, they definitely have a death wish and I'm bloody in it.

They square up to the police, ready to go head-to-head, and I'm thinking "Fantastic, they're going to shoot us all and bury us at sea."

So, me, being the biggest lunatic of them all, stepped in front of the officers with my hands up, trying to calm things down. "Let's all take a breath here, yeah?" I say, while dragging my six stubborn stupid friends backward, inch by inch, and trying to avoid getting us all shot.

Finally, I get everyone to back away slowly, and then, as soon as there's a bit of space, we bolt. We're running like bloody hell, sprinting down the street as if our lives depend on it—because, well, they probably do.

And as I'm running, all I can think is, "If I survive this, I'm never, ever going on holiday with these maniacs again."

What happened next was truly the cherry on top of this chaotic night. So after running like madmen, we finally start slowing down, trying to catch our breath.

Its pitch black, we're all out of breath, and we decide it's best to keep a bit quieter to avoid, you know, getting shot at again. We're creeping along, trying to blend into the shadows, when one of the lads suddenly stops and says, "Wait... where's Dave?"

And then we hear it—a faint, desperate voice calling out from somewhere nearby, "Help! Help! Help!" We look around, and there, down an open sewer drain, is Dave, waving his hands and looking like a proper mess. He'd managed to fall straight into the sewer!

If I tell you I was on the floor laughing, I mean it—absolutely doubled over. We finally haul him out, and he's covered head-to-toe in god-knows-what, looking like he's been through a mud wrestling match with a skunk.

Bruised, battered, and definitely in need of a tetanus shot, he's dripping with what can only be described as sewer soup. The rest of us are trying to catch our breath from laughing so hard while Dave's standing there, fuming, smelling like a dumpster, muttering something about never trusting us again.

And let's just say, that night, the lad got the first bath he'd had in years!

Chapter 71: The Day Everything Changed: A Heart Attack at 70

August 2023. It's a day I'll never forget, a day that changed everything. Whether you call it a bad day or a good one depends on how you see it, I suppose. For me, it was the day I had a heart attack. A heart attack—me, of all people. It hit me like a freight train, blindsiding me completely. I've always thought of myself as invincible. How could I not? I've lived a life of discipline: never smoked, never drank, eaten organic food, exercised every single day, and practised martial arts for as long as I can remember. I've always done everything "right."

And yet, there I was, lying helpless, my chest gripped by pain. It didn't seem real, couldn't be real. How could this happen to me? But then, the truth hit me like the pain that had floored me—this wasn't about my choices. It was in my blood, passed down through my family. Inherited. Go figure. Seventy years of thinking I could outrun fate, and here I was.

As I lay there, trying to come to terms with what was happening, my thoughts weren't about me. No, they were about my children. I could see their faces in my mind, could feel their worry, their fear. I kept thinking, "What if I don't survive this? What will they do without me? How will they cope?" That thought was more painful than anything my body was going through.

You see, my life has never really been about me. It's always been about them—my children, my family. I've dedicated everything to making their lives better, being their rock. And now, in what could have been my final moments, all I could think of was the weight of what they might carry if I was gone.

I knew Jackie was watching over me from above, and I felt her presence in my heart. Maybe that's what kept me fighting, kept me holding on. But even now, as I recover, the weight of that day lingers. It wasn't just the physical pain or the shock of it all—it was the realisation of how fragile everything is. Life, no matter how carefully we live it, is so uncertain.

I've always been strong for everyone else. But that day? That day reminded me how much I need them, too.

Chapter 72: Why I'm Writing This

In August 2023, I had a heart attack. It shook me more deeply than you might realise—not just because of what I went through, but because I kept thinking about how it might affect each of you. There were moments when I wasn't sure I'd make it, and it made me realise how much I needed to tell you what's in my heart. I never really had the chance to tell you just how much you all mean to me.

Chapter 73: A lasting love letter

As I lie here thinking about my life, I find myself wondering if I should write this letter to you, even though I'm still here. I know you might not want to hear what I'm about to say, and I can imagine it may bring tears. But I need you to know, with all my heart, how much I love each of you.

It's been over a year since I had the heart attack, and I know how deeply it affected you all. I am beyond grateful for how each of you rallied around me, for the strength, love, and kindness you showed. You were there for me in every way possible, and I can't begin to tell you how much that meant.

Please know that I will always be here for you, in every way I can, in spirit and in love. I know each of you so well—your kindness, your courage, your hearts. There's one promise I need from you: promise me that you'll always be there for each other, just as you were there for me. Carry forward the love, strength, and unity that bind us. You all have a strength in you that comes straight from your mother—her heart, her resilience, her spirit.

Remember, you're never alone. You have each other, and you carry my love with you, always.

Life is full of surprises, and if there's one thing I've truly come to understand, it's this: enjoy the journey. It's wild, unpredictable, sometimes messy, and breathtakingly beautiful in ways you don't always see coming. Each twist and turn, each unexpected moment—it's all part of this precious, fleeting ride we're on.

I don't know how much time I have left on this earth, but what I do know is that each day is a gift, a chance to live fully, love deeply, and leave nothing unspoken. Life doesn't wait, and neither should you. Live each day as if it's your last, because there's magic in the present—in the laughter, the joy, the simple conversations, and even in the quiet pauses. There's magic in each connection you make, each moment you spend with the people you love, and in every single breath you take.

So, please, my dear ones, embrace it all. Savour every experience, every laugh, every tear, and every triumph. Never hold back, never wait to say "I love you," and never forget that life is happening right here, right now. Let yourself feel deeply, love fully, and chase every moment of joy that comes your way. Because, in the end, it's these moments, the memories you make, that will carry you and keep you close to the ones you love, even long after I'm gone.

I write this with tears in my eyes, knowing I may not be here to watch you, my beloved children and your beautiful children, grow into all you're meant to be. It fills me with such sorrow to say these words, yet please carry this truth with you always: I am with you, now and forever. I will be watching over you, guiding you, and holding you close, even if you can't see me there.

My deepest wish is that, when you think of me, you'll remember the laughter we shared, the love that filled our lives, and the adventures we were blessed to experience together. I hope those memories bring you comfort and warmth, like a soft light in your heart, reminding you that my love surrounds you always.

Please know, with everything I am, just how much I love you.

Words will never be enough, but I love you beyond what I could ever say or show. I will be by your side, by your mum's side, protecting you, guiding you, and celebrating every triumph with you, every single step of the way. I want nothing more than for you to have lives overflowing with love, laughter, and the peace and joy that you deserve.

Carry my love with you always, and know that in every moment of your life, I am there, holding you close, so proud of you, and wishing you the most beautiful journey life has to offer.

I know that saying goodbye brings sadness, but please don't mourn my passing. Instead, celebrate my life—the memories we made, the laughter we shared, the love that will always connect us. Know that I am with you, always, right there in your heart. In every cherished memory, every smile, and every moment of joy, I live on with you. Let my love be a comfort and a reminder that, no matter what, I am by your side, just as I have always been.

Chapter 74: Let the Magic Begin: Embracing Every Moment Together

Hold on a second—I'm still here, and there's so much life left to live! There are still plenty of adventures ahead, so let's embrace every one of them together. Life is magical, filled with surprises we haven't yet discovered, and moments waiting to be celebrated. Let's cherish it all, laugh often, and make the most of every single day. So, let the magic begin!

Chapter 75: A 12-Year-Old's Wild Crossbow Adventure

So, picture this: it's about 60 years ago. TVs were black and white, and if you were lucky enough to have one, the screen was the size of a shoebox. There was a show called William Tell, all about this guy back in the time of knights, dragons, and King Arthur, forced to shoot an apple off his son's head with a crossbow. I, being the aspiring young madman I was at age 12, watched that and thought, "Now that's the kind of skill I need in my life!"

Back then, you could buy almost anything in the shops, including mini crossbows. These things were metal — looked really real — and they fired little arrows with rubber suction cups on the ends. The arrows would stick to the wall like you'd stuck it there with glue. "Safe for kids!" they said. If it had even a shred of rubber on it, it was practically health and safety approved.

Anyway, naturally, I got one. But here's where things took a turn. Just having a crossbow wasn't enough for me. No, no, no — I needed the full William

Tell experience. And for that, I needed a target. Of course who else but my cousin. Somehow, I convinced him to balance an apple on his head, while I took aim. Now, most kids would stop there, right? Not me. Because I was... well, let's just say I was a "creative thinker."

So what did I do? I pulled off the rubber tip, of course, and gave that arrow a little extra "sharpening." What's an archer without a pointy arrow? I figured, "If William Tell can do it with a real arrow, then so can I!" And with a grin, I lined up my shot, barely able to see through the crossbow's "sights" and my sheer determination.

Then, I took the shot. The arrow whistled through the air, my cousin's eyes nearly bulged out of his head... Right into the apple. A perfect hit! My cousin exhaled so hard he nearly blew the apple off his own head.

So kids, take it from me: Do not try this at home. Or, if you do, maybe leave the rubber tip on!

Chapter 76: Facing the Unbearable: My Journey through Pain and Silence

Life is so unpredictable. I believe we're tested and challenged every day, and this was definitely one of those times. Fifteen years ago, I found myself in agonising pain. I had just returned from Salt Lake City, my back getting worse by the day. My brother had passed away, and I could barely manage to help carry his coffin. Like a fool, I didn't get it checked out.

Not long after, I was at home, in the hallway, when the pain hit hard. I couldn't move, completely overwhelmed. The day I met Richard, who would become my future son-in-law, I initially thought it was our first meeting. However, when I spoke with Gema, she reminded me that I had actually met Richard weeks earlier. I remember shouting up to Gema, "You need to call an ambulance!" For someone who hates doctors, that was saying a lot. Gema quickly called 999, and within minutes, the ambulance arrived.

The paramedics were amazing, calm and supportive. They assessed the situation and said, "Alright, we need to get you into the ambulance." I immediately replied, "Don't touch me!" Even the slightest movement sent pain shooting through my entire body.

But, of course, I had to get into that ambulance somehow. It ended up taking a full three hours — inch by inch, a careful process to avoid the agony of movement — before I finally made it inside. They showed incredible patience, and I'll never forget it.

Eventually, I was finally in the ambulance, but then came the next hurdle: "Now you have to sit down," they told me. "Are you kidding?" I thought. I could hardly move, but they pumped me full of painkillers until I was in another world, practically floating, and then strapped me in.

We arrived at the hospital, and after four hours I finally got a bed. I waited all night, and it wasn't until the following morning that a doctor came by. He barely examined me, asked me to describe the pain, and quickly concluded, "Sounds like sciatica." And that was it—they sent me home. No X-ray, no scan, nothing. Would you believe that?

When I finally got home, the pain was unbearable. I need you to understand—no position, no amount of shifting or adjusting, brought any relief. It was relentless, an agony that just wouldn't let up. We called the doctor, and she was amazing; she actually came to the house and gave me the strongest painkillers possible. But even those didn't touch the pain.

My sons, bless them, brought a mattress downstairs so I wouldn't have to move up and down. But as the days dragged on, the pain only got worse, gnawing at me. I started to feel like a burden to my family. I'd always been the one to take care of them, and now here I was, helpless. I didn't want to be there; the frustration and helplessness were overwhelming.

I asked the doctor to arrange a CAT scan, desperate to find out what was really happening. At first, she refused, but I didn't back down. I kept pushing, and finally, an appointment was arranged. I just needed answers—some way to understand and hopefully put an end to this constant pain.

The doctor finally came with the results. She explained that my nerves were pressing together in a way that would only make the pain worsen over time. Then came the blow: "You may never walk again."

I couldn't believe it. "Are you kidding me?" I thought, stunned. It was too much to process. The pain was already overwhelming, and now my mind couldn't wrap around her words. It felt surreal, like I was trapped in a nightmare or maybe I'd misheard. Did she really say that? It was almost too much to accept.

I didn't tell the kids; I didn't want them to worry. I needed time to process it myself. But as the days went on, the pain only got worse. It was constant—every second, every minute, and every hour. The agony was relentless, a weight pressing down on me day and night.

When no one was around, I'd lie in bed in tears, trying to hold it together barely able to cope in the quiet moments alone. I felt trapped in my own body, each day blending into the next, the pain unyielding.

Having practised martial arts my whole life, I knew the power of resilience and focus. In my darkest moments, I remembered Bruce Lee's story: how he'd broken his back and was told he'd never walk or fight again. But he defied the odds through sheer mental strength and relentless discipline, proving everyone wrong by not only walking again but fighting, too. Inspired by his story, lying in bed in indescribable pain, I decided I had to fight back with everything I had.

Every night, even as pain tore through me, I closed my eyes and saw myself running, leaping, flipping through the air. I pictured myself walking without pain, my body completely healed. No position could ease the agony, but I was determined. Every night, I forced myself to see that version of me—strong, whole, and unbroken. The pain was relentless, and at times, it seemed impossible, but I wouldn't let go.

Then, after six gruelling months, something happened that felt like a miracle. One day, I shifted ever so slightly and found a position where, for the first time, the pain stopped. It was only a fraction of an angle, but it was enough—a glimpse of hope. Day by day, inch by inch, the pain began to loosen its grip. And I kept pushing, refusing to let go of that vision of myself healed and whole. Gradually, the pain faded, until one day, it was completely gone.

When I went to physio, they gave me exercises to rebuild my strength, but I knew the real work had started in my mind, in those countless nights I fought against the pain with everything I had. It was nothing short of a miracle—but one I fought for, one I willed into existence.

They told me to take it slow. Did I listen? Not a chance. I'd been given a second chance, and there was no way I was wasting it by holding back. I threw myself back into life with everything I had. I returned to martial arts, determined to rebuild the strength that pain had tried to take from me.

Then I pushed even harder. I bought a program called Insanity—and it was just that: pure, brutal insanity. Every session was a battle, the kind of training that only the fearless would dare attempt. But I wasn't backing down. For three relentless months, I took on that challenge, day after day, proving that I could go further than anyone thought possible.

That was 15 years ago. Looking back, I can still feel the rawness of those days—months of agony, six months of living through hell, fighting through every second with nothing but my own will to carry me. But it wasn't just survival; it was rebirth. I faced down the impossible and didn't just win—I came back stronger than ever

And here's the truth—I didn't fight through all of that just for me. I did it for my family. I wanted them to see that no matter how dark things get, you never give up. You don't surrender to pain, and you don't back down from what feels impossible. I wanted to show them that strength isn't about never falling; it's about getting back up, fighting through every inch of it, and coming out stronger.

I needed them to know that we don't let life's hardest moments define us. We face them head-on, for ourselves, for the people we love, and for the future we're building. So I fought, not just to survive, but to live fully, to be present, and to be the person they could rely on, no matter what. For them, I refused to quit. For them, I kept pushing forward. Because that's what it means to truly fight—to keep going, even when every part of you wants to stop.

Chapter 77: Bonfire Night Gone Wrong; The Sparkler Mishap That Thankfully Left No Mark!

Ah, the epic sparkler fiasco with Gema! One of those nights where everything that could go wrong absolutely did. It was bonfire night, and we'd already set off all the big fireworks, down to the last little sparklers. Gema, about three years old, was in her element, waving her sparkler around like she was painting in the air.

And then... It happened. In one swift, unplanned move, she somehow manages to tap the burning end right onto the bridge of her nose. I freeze, thinking "Well, that's it. I've officially won the Worst Dad of the Year award."

Naturally, Jackie's upstairs, out of commission with a cold, leaving me, of all people, as the "responsible adult." So here I am, scooping up a slightly singed Gema, muttering, "Its fine, its fine!" while she's looking at me like I've just ruined her life. I rush her to the bathroom, plop her in the bath, and start splashing water on her nose, hoping this tiny red mark will just...

disappear. Nope! The little burn is as clear as day, sitting right there on her nose, taunting me.

Meanwhile, all I can think is, Jackie is going to kill me. Finally, Jackie drags herself downstairs, takes one look at Gema's sparkler-scarred nose, and just lets out a deep sigh, muttering, "Oh no... not again." Because, of course, somehow, this wasn't my first parenting disaster!

Over time, the mark faded completely—no scar at all, thank goodness! You'd never even know it happened.

Chapter 78: Bournemouth Bound and Broke; How I Got Talked into a Rodeo by My Scheming Wife

So, Jackie, my dear partner-in-crime, has a knack for getting me into trouble. And this day was no exception. We'd booked a holiday in Bournemouth, all excited, looking forward to some sun, sea, and relaxation. I had this convertible—1360cc, smooth as butter—so off we go, cruising along, wind in our hair. What could possibly go wrong, right? Well, buckle up.

We roll into Bournemouth, and just as I'm thinking "Ah, the good life," the car suddenly loses all power. Dead. We roll to a stop right outside a BMW garage, of all places. Perfect timing, right? We head inside, chat to the mechanic, and he gives it a look. "Your clutch is gone, mate," he says, straight-faced. I'm thinking, "Well, fantastic!" He tells us it'll be £45. Now, 55 years ago, £45 was practically a small fortune. This was like blowing the entire holiday fund before we even started. So we leave the car, spirits low, and go wandering through town while it gets fixed.

And, of course, it's bucketing down with rain. I'm trying to stay positive, which is hard when you've basically got no money left and you're soaked to the skin. We haven't even checked into the guesthouse yet. But then the clouds start to part, and the sun peeks out, like the universe is finally giving us a break. We stumble upon this park with a massive banner that reads: "RODEO! £300 Prize for Longest Ride!"

Jackie, bless her, looks at me with that gleam in her eye and says, "You should do it!" I say, "Who, me? Are you mad? I'm not getting thrown off a horse for a laugh." But Jackie's like, "Oh, come on, think of the money!" She's practically bouncing with excitement, and somehow, I let her talk me into it. I'm trying to picture myself wrangling a bucking bronco, wondering if I'll end up in the hospital… or worse. For a brief moment, I suggest Jackie try it instead. But that idea dies on the spot. No way, not in her plans.

So there I was, on holiday, about to test my skills as an amateur cowboy, all because Jackie thought it'd be "a great idea." Turns out, the only rodeo was me just trying to keep up with her crazy ideas.

So, here we go. We stroll into the park and head over to where the rodeo is set up. There's a guy there, looking the part with a big cowboy hat and boots that have probably never seen a horse in their life. He greets us in the thickest American accent you've ever heard, like he just stepped out of a Wild West movie. I'm thinking, "Hang on a minute, isn't that a Manchester accent sneaking through?"

But he's committed. "Y'all here to ride the bull?" he drawls, tipping his hat like he's in a saloon. I glance at Jackie, who's already beaming with excitement and giving me the thumbs up. I sigh and say, "Yeah, I guess I'm here to give it a go." So he puts my name down and tells us to come back at 3 o'clock. I nod, but in my head, I'm already wondering if I should book a hospital room instead of a guesthouse. Jackie's practically bouncing, like I've just signed up for the Olympics or something.

We walk away, and I say to her, "You know he's about as American as a meat pie, right?" But she's too busy laughing, probably already imagining me being launched off that bull like a sack of potatoes. 3 o'clock couldn't come fast enough... or maybe too fast!

So now the sun's out, it's a warm, beautiful day, and Jackie's practically glowing, like she can already see those prize winnings in her bank account. Meanwhile, I'm over here wondering if I'll need therapy after this. How did I let myself get talked into this? I'm about to climb onto a bucking death machine, and all because Jackie's counting imaginary money.

We head back over to Mr. "Howdy Partner," still rocking that fake American accent, who tells me I'll be up in just a minute. I glance over to see what I'm actually supposed to ride, and there it is: a tiny, ridiculous-looking mechanical bull sitting on a small mat. It's barely the size of a cardboard box, bobbing up and down like it's just learned to float. I'm thinking "That's it? That's the "rodeo" challenge? Easy money!"

I turn to Jackie, feeling just a bit braver, and say, "What could go wrong, eh?" She's smiling like she's at a Las Vegas slot machine that's about to pay out. Meanwhile, in my head, I'm still halfway between thinking, "I got this" and "Where's the nearest hospital?"

So, the park's absolutely packed, people crowded around like it's the Superbowl, all of them waiting to see someone get launched sky-high. My name's called over the loudspeaker: "All the way from sunny Liverpool... Mr. Geoffrey Loveday!" I raise my hands, taking in the applause like a rock star, trying to ignore the fact that I might not live to see the end of this.

As I strut toward the "arena," I spot an ambulance parked nearby. Then, this guy sidles up to me with a grim look and goes, "Good luck, mate. Be careful—the last guy got knocked out cold. That's why the ambulance is here." Perfect! Nothing like hearing about potential brain damage to boost your confidence.

Finally, I get a good look at this "box" they're keeping the horse in. I thought it'd be a cute mechanical pony or something, but no, it's a massive wooden contraption with these horrendous thuds and screams coming from inside. This thing sounds like a haunted house crossed with a tornado.

The rodeo guy waves me over, giving me the instructions of a lifetime: "Just climb up the ladder, get over the edge, sit yourself on the horse, and get comfy for the ride of your life." "Ride of my life?" I think. More like the end of my life. But somehow, I'm still climbing that ladder.

I reach the top and peer down into the box. There it is—a gigantic, wild-eyed horse. No saddle, no reins, nothing but a big, splintery beam right at head height. The horse is on its back legs, looking like it wants out more than I do. I'm sitting there, trying to get comfy on what feels like a bare tree trunk, holding on to the sides, and the guy shouts, "No, not like that! Are you ready?"

"Not bloody ready!" I yell, but before I can say anything else, he bellows, "Let it go!"

The doors swing open, and the horse bolts out of there like it's seen a ghost, galloping full speed into the arena. Only one slight problem—I'm still in the box, clutching the beams like a terrified koala! The horse has taken off without me, and I'm left there dangling, looking like I've just survived a tornado.

The crowd goes absolutely silent. All I hear is the announcer mumbling, "Uh... would you believe it, folks? He's done an invisible rodeo ride!"

I finally climb down, wondering how I'm going to explain this to Jackie, who's probably out there thinking I just won us £300. Instead, I've managed to become Bournemouth's first invisible cowboy. Ride of my life? More like the pride of my life just ran off into the distance without me

Oh, I can practically hear her now. Jackie's standing there, hands on her hips, trying not to laugh but absolutely failing

Alright, here's how Jackie really hit me with it:

Jackie's standing there, arms crossed, trying (and failing) to keep a straight face. She walks over, looks me up and down, and just lets me have it:

"Well, that was quite a performance, Mr. Rodeo Star! Should I start calling you 'The Great Invisible Cowboy'? I think you were on that horse for a record-breaking zero seconds!"

Then, she leans in and says, "You know, I was planning on spending that prize money, but I guess I'll settle for the priceless memory of watching you sit there clinging to the box while your 'ride' ran off into the sunset."

And just when I thought she was done, she gave me a smirk and said, "Next time you want to impress me, maybe try something safer. Like, I don't know... bingo?"

Exactly! I look at her, absolutely gobsmacked, and say, "Are you serious? Impress you? This whole disaster was your brilliant idea! You're the one who convinced me to climb up there like some wannabe cowboy!"

She just shrugs, barely holding back a laugh, and says, "Oh, come on, it was a great idea! I thought you'd be up there like John Wayne!"

I'm shaking my head, muttering, "John Wayne? More like Gone with the Wind!" Meanwhile, she's practically in stitches, saying, "Oh, please, you're the one who walked up there all hero-like! Don't act like you didn't love it!"

Honestly, this woman! She talks me into it, stands there laughing while I nearly become a human cannonball, and then has the nerve to say I was trying to impress her! Unbelievable. I swear, next holiday, we're sticking to mini golf.

The one silver lining? By the time we stumbled back from my Invisible Rodeo debacle, Jackie had completely forgotten about the car. We picked it up without her even mentioning the whole clutch catastrophe. Talk about a miracle!

And from there, things took a serious turn for the better. We ended up having the most amazing holiday—no more rodeo stunts, no more broken clutches, just sunshine, seaside, and a lot of laughs. Well, mostly Jackie laughing at my "cowboy" skills, but still.

By the end, she couldn't even bring herself to complain about the repair bill, which, given everything else, felt like a small miracle in itself.

There was more to come on the holiday, read on how Jackie talked me into another adventure.

Chapter 79: How I Nearly Drowned Trying to be Superman

So, there I was, just another "normal" day where I barely escaped death. How I survive, I honestly have no clue. Jackie and I were on holiday, right? Gorgeous beach, sun blazing, waves gently lapping the shore. Jackie's laid out in the sand, sunning herself, looking like some sun goddess, while I'm nearby flexing my muscles like I'm about to be cast in Baywatch.

And then—I spotted it. A little boy, lying on a lilo, drifting out to sea. His dad is on the shore, standing there frozen, looking like he's seen a ghost, and meanwhile, the child's bobbing out like he's on some one-way trip to America. He's half a mile out already!

I leap to my feet and say to Jackie, "This is a job for Superman!" And before she can say, "Oh, here we go," I'm off. I run into the sea in slow motion (at least in my head) and dive in, swimming with all the strength of an action hero. But here's the thing—the kid's moving faster than I am, getting farther and farther away.

Now he's about a mile out. But I keep going. I'm thinking, "This is it. I'm going to be a hero. The papers are going to love this." And then—wham!—I got the worst cramp of my life. Feels like my leg is about to pop right off. I'm kicking, flailing, and gulping saltwater, thinking, "This is it. I'm gonna go down trying to be a hero. I'm gonna drown here in three feet of water."

But then I see another guy in the water. I shout, "Hey, go save the kid!" He looks at me, completely out of breath, and shouts back, "I can't! I'm dying out here!" Just as we're both about to become floating corpses a little boy about seven years old, swims past us both. I swear, he's practically doing the butterfly stroke. He zooms out, grabs the lilo, snatches the drifting child, and just casually swims back to shore like he's on a warm-up lap. Not even breathing hard.

Meanwhile, there I am, two miles out, legs like concrete blocks, cramp so bad I'm rethinking my life choices, and all I can do is try not to swallow half the ocean. I managed to flop my way back eventually, gasping, half-dead. Jackie's there waiting, doesn't look the least bit impressed. She just hands me a towel and says, that wasn't very clever was it?

I'm standing there, dripping wet, lungs full of seawater, and I just stare at her, thinking "Are you serious right now? This was your idea! You're the one who convinced me I was some sort of Baywatch hero!"

But no, she's just enjoying the show, looking at me like, "Well, maybe next time you'll think twice before jumping into the ocean without a plan." Unbelievable. Only Jackie could make me feel like the one who lacked common sense in this situation.

The moral of the story? With Jackie around, I don't need to sign up for extreme sports. My daily life is already an adventure, thanks to her "brilliant" ideas!

Chapter 80: Nightmare on Cliffside: How Jackie's Adventures Followed Me to My Dreams!

So there I was, sound asleep, finally getting some rest after that whirlwind of a holiday Jackie had me on. But no—my brain apparently thought I hadn't had enough of her "adventures" and decided to give me one more... in my dreams.

In this nightmare, we're back on the beach, and I'm stretched out, trying to relax. I think I deserve it after the invisible rodeo and the whole drowning fiasco, right? But then Jackie turns to me with that mischievous look that can only mean one thing: trouble. She leans over and says, "Geoffrey, how about one more little adventure?"

Now, you'd think I'd know better, even in a dream. But I find myself nodding, and before I can even protest, she's dragging me along. Apparently, she's found this "scenic cliff trail" she thinks would be "fun" to explore.

Next thing I know, we're clambering up this trail, but it's more like scaling a mountain. I'm practically crawling on my hands and knees, every step wobbling, while Jackie's just powering ahead like we're out for a stroll. At one point, I glance down, and it's just a drop into nothingness. My heart's pounding, but Jackie's all smiles, calling out, "Come on, Geoffrey! You're so slow!"

Just as I think we're done, Jackie finds a narrow little path leading up even higher. And she's insisting we climb it! Now I'm clinging to this boulder for dear life, looking around for rescue helicopters, and Jackie's just dangling her legs over the edge, having the time of her life.

I wake up in a cold sweat, my heart still racing. Jackie's fast asleep beside me, peaceful as can be, while I'm lying there thinking, "She's even got me cliff-diving in my dreams!" Honestly, after this holiday, I don't know what's real anymore—just that I need a vacation from our actual vacation!

Chapter 81: How My Romantic Horseback Ride Turned into a High-Speed Nightmare

So, here's the scene: Jackie and I had just started dating, and I knew she loved horses. In my head, I thought, I'll impress her! Take her horseback riding! What could go wrong? Never mind that I'd never even touched a horse before, but, of course, I had visions of myself as some kind of John Wayne.

We arrive at the stables on a gorgeous day, and I'm already feeling pretty smug. We're handed two horses, and before I can even ask about a riding lesson, they just toss us up on these beasts and send us out into the countryside. Just the two of us, with me—Captain Cowboy Wannabe—winging it for dear life.

Now, Jackie's an experienced rider, so she's trotting along, totally at ease, while I'm sitting on top of this massive creature that seems far too aware I have no clue what I'm doing. I'm holding onto the reins like they're a lifeline, whispering, "Easy, boy," and praying it understands English.

Jackie turns around and says, "Are you okay back there?" And in my head, I'm screaming, "No, I'm definitely not okay! I need someone to hold my hand! Or better yet, get me down from here!" But out loud, I give her a cool little nod, like I've got this all under control.

Then, suddenly, her horse starts trotting faster, and of course, mine decides to follow. So now we're picking up speed, and I'm bouncing up and down like I'm riding a bucking bronco. At one point, I'm practically airborne, clutching onto the saddle for dear life, trying not to look as terrified as I feel. Meanwhile, Jackie's ahead, looking all graceful and natural, like she's auditioning for Hello magazine.

I try to regain some dignity and steer the horse a bit, but it's like this thing has a mind of its own. We round a corner, and my horse decides its snack time, stops dead, and starts munching on some bushes. I'm half hanging off the side, trying to pull it back onto the trail, while Jackie's stifling laughter, calling back, "Need some help, cowboy?"

At this point, I'm one step away from a full-blown panic attack. And just when I thought I'd made it through the worst of it, my horse suddenly decides it's auditioning for the Grand National. Out of nowhere, it bolts, tearing off across the countryside like a bat out of hell. This thing is moving like it's got somewhere very important to be, and I'm hanging on for dear life, bouncing around like a rag doll.

My feet are barely in the stirrups, and I'm clinging to the saddle with a death grip, wondering if this is how it ends. Jackie's up ahead, riding along gracefully, completely oblivious, while I'm back here, practically flying. The countryside's a blur, the wind's roaring in my ears, and all I can think is, I really should have paid extra for that lesson.

I pass Jackie so fast like I'm auditioning for the bloody Grand National. The horse is going so fast I feel like I'm in a time warp. My hat's gone, my pride's gone, and any shred of dignity I had has definitely gone. Meanwhile, Jackie finally notices I'm nowhere in sight, and just sees this wild scene: me, eyes wide as saucers, gripping the horse like it's about to launch me into orbit.

Finally, after what feels like an eternity, the horse decides it's had enough and slows down. I'm shaking, heart racing, trying to catch my breath as Jackie catches up, and looking like she's trying really hard not to burst into laughter.

She grins and says, "Had a nice ride?"

I'm too busy catching my breath to even respond, but I think I managed to nod. And that was the day I learned that trying to impress Jackie might just lead to a heart attack.

Why does this always happen to me? Honestly, I couldn't tell you if I tried! Every time I try to do something impressive, romantic, or even slightly adventurous, it all goes sideways faster than you can say, "Hold on tight!" It's like the universe has a special comedy show starring me as the punchline.

Maybe its fate, maybe it's just my incredible knack for disaster, but whatever it is, I end up hanging on for dear life while everyone else—especially Jackie—has a front-row seat for the spectacle. I guess some people are just born to have things go smoothly, and others, well... we're here to keep things interesting.

Chapter 82: The day I knocked myself unconscious: Everyone was laughing except Jackie – she never spoke to me for two weeks

This is yet another example of things spiralling completely out of control—and, yes, I'm convinced it's Jackie's fault. It always starts with one of her "brilliant" ideas, and somehow, I'm the one ending up in hot water while she just smiles and shrugs.

So, one day, I'm singing in the bath, minding my own business, thinking it's just me and the shampoo bottles. I get out, and there's Jackie, looking at me like she's just discovered Elvis himself in our bathroom. She says, "You've got a great voice!" Now, if you know Jackie, you know this can only mean one thing: trouble. I barely have time to grab a towel before she's got this wild idea that I should be a singer.

"You're kidding, right?" I say, but no, she's not. A few days later, somehow, I signed up to perform at a singing competition at a local hotel. I've got six songs to learn, my nerves are in shreds, and Jackie's only words of encouragement are, "You'll be fine." Famous last words.

The big day arrives, and I'm absolutely petrified, sweating like I'm in a sauna. Jackie's just there, grinning ear-to-ear, convinced I'm the next Frank Sinatra. I get up there, belt out my songs, and wouldn't you know it—I don't even make it to the finals. I'm just relieved to escape with my dignity, but Jackie's looking like she can't believe it. Then, as we're leaving, the hotel manager catches us and says, "You should have won! Come back next week, and you'll take the prize."

Well, Jackie's absolutely delighted. "See? I told you!" she says, and suddenly, I'm rehearsing all over again, and now I'm starting to think maybe she's right. So I go back the next week, give it my all, and sure enough—I win! Jackie's over the moon, already spending the prize money in her mind. She's bought imaginary new furniture, a holiday, and the works.

Now, I'm booked for the final at the Mersey View Hotel in Runcorn, where the prize is a whopping £1,000. Jackie's got the entire amount mentally accounted for before I even step on stage.

But, of course, things don't go according to plan. What happened next? Well, let's just say, if you thought the singing was a twist, wait until you hear what went down at that final...

So, it's the big day—the final. I'm already a bundle of nerves, but Jackie? She's treated this like the social event of the century. She hasn't come alone, oh no. She's invited everyone she knows, probably a few people she doesn't know, and I swear, if she could have somehow sent a private jet for the Pope, he'd be there, too.

I walk into the venue, and there it is: a row of tables lined up around the dance floor, every single one packed with people who've come to see me. Jackie's at the front, practically vibrating with excitement, grinning like she's my manager and my number one fan all rolled into one.

Now, picture this: there's the stage, with two absolutely massive speakers on either side. These things are about the size of a small house. And to add to the stage drama, there's a set of steps leading down from the stage to the dance floor, almost like a ramp to disaster waiting to happen.

I'm standing there, heart pounding, looking at the setup and wondering, "What have I gotten myself into?" Jackie catches my eye, gives me the biggest thumbs up, mouthing, "You've got this!" Meanwhile, I'm not sure if I'm about to sing my heart out or trip over my own feet in front of the entire town.

And believe me, the way things go with Jackie around, anything could happen next...

Alright, get ready for this one. So, I'm at this talent show, right? Third in line, ready to absolutely crush "Can't Smile Without You" by Barry Manilow. And to add a bit of mystique, I'm going by this stage name: "Toni Denton." Don't ask me why—it just sounded classy and I thought it would give me a little extra edge, you know? So they call out, "Toni Denton to the stage!" and I strut up there like I'm headlining Madison Square Garden.

They pass me the mic, the music starts, and I'm in full Barry mode. I'm talking about a serious singer's face, eyes closed, full body sway—just pouring my heart into this thing. And then I walk straight into the bloody speaker. Like, not a gentle bump—no, I basically tackle it. Suddenly, I'm airborne, practically doing a backflip. The mic flies one way, I go flying the other, and I hit the ground like a sack of potatoes. Out cold.

I come to maybe thirty seconds later, all confused, but in my dazed state, I grab the mic, get up, and jump back into the song…only I'm in the wrong key. But at this point, I'm too rattled to even realise it. Meanwhile, the audience is losing it—they're cracking up, thinking this is some bizarre comedy act. I'm trying to keep it together, but then I look out and catch Jackie's eye. The look on her face! Let's just say it didn't exactly boost my confidence.

And naturally, I didn't win. Not even close. I walk off stage, feeling like I've just been through a one-man circus act—bruised, battered, and completely out of pride. Jackie? She doesn't say a single word. For two whole weeks, I'm met with stone-cold silence. And here's the kicker: this entire disaster was her idea!

One minute, I'm harmlessly singing in the bath, thinking I'm alone with my shampoo audience, and the next, I'm Toni Denton, airborne off a stage, giving the audience a show that probably got mistaken for slapstick comedy.

If there's one thing I've learned, it's this: whenever Jackie has a "brilliant idea," I should skip the pep talk and go straight for the first-aid kit. Her "plans" come with a side order of public humiliation and just enough injury to make it unforgettable.

So next time, I'll be strapping on a helmet, bringing a stretcher, and maybe calling in a medic ahead of time—because with Jackie's ideas, you never know what you're signing up for!

Chapter 83: Never again; But somehow I don't think so

Ah, here we go again—another one of Jackie's "brilliant" ideas. What could possibly go wrong, right? I must really enjoy suffering, because somehow, I'm saying this again. Honestly, I might as well wear a leash around my neck that Jackie can tug on every time she cooks up a new way to ruin my day.

So, we're in Bournemouth, and after the rodeo debacle and the near-death ocean rescue, I'm thinking Jackie's probably ready to take it easy. But no, Jackie doesn't do it easily. She clearly wants to up the stakes. We're lounging by the pool when I spot it: a massive diving board. And not just any diving board—it's got three levels. The first is a nice, low one, like it's for beginners. The second is higher, a bit challenging. And the third? It's the death-defying leap of doom.

I'm casually glancing at it, just looking, and Jackie catches me. You'd think she'd let it go, but no. She leans over with that mischievous glint in her eye and says, "Bet you can't dive from the top board."

Now, you have to understand something. Jackie knows I'm petrified of heights. She's known this since the day we met. But of course, she says it like it's nothing, like she's daring me to tie my shoes. "Of course I can!" I say, because apparently, I have zero self-control.

Jackie smirks. "Oh, I don't think so," she says. And just like that, I'm already halfway mentally committing to this madness. She's good, isn't she? Playing me like a fiddle.

"It's not even that high!" she says, nodding toward the board. "Look, there are children jumping from the top! What do you think—too scared? I mean, it's fine if you are…"

And here I go, falling for it yet again. "No, I'm not scared!" I snap, even though I'm already sweating at the thought. She's planted the seed, and now I'm climbing up the ladder in my head. What happens next? Well, you're about to find out just how far Jackie's "ideas" can push me this time…

As I'm climbing the ladder, I can already feel the wind—and the whole thing swaying beneath me. It's like the bloody ladder itself is having second thoughts. I try to convince myself I'm fine. First section? Not too bad. I think, "This isn't so high, I can do this." Then I reach the second section, and my confidence is starting to wobble as much as the ladder.

Finally, I'm climbing the last ladder to the top. By now, I'm pretty sure I'm ascending directly into the clouds. I step onto the diving board, and that's when it hits me: this isn't just a "high dive." No, this is a death-defying leap of lunacy.

I shuffle forward, my legs turning to jelly, and then I make the mistake—the massive mistake—of looking down. Big mistake. From up there, the pool looks like a tiny postage stamp. It doesn't even look like water anymore—just a blue dot mocking me from below. Honestly, it's like doing a bungee jump... but without the bungee cord. Or a parachute. Or a safety net. Just you, gravity, and the terrifying knowledge that this was all Jackie's idea.

I stand there, heart pounding, thinking, No way. Absolutely no way. I am NOT jumping off this thing without a net—or, frankly, a rescue team waiting at the bottom.

I turn around, ready to retreat like a sensible human being, and as I look back toward the ladder, I make the mistake of catching Jackie's eye. She's down there, arms crossed, with the biggest smirk on her face. She's loving every second of my panic. "Go on, then!" she shouts, practically cackling.

At that moment, I realised something: I can't back down now. Not with Jackie down there, probably ready to tell everyone I chickened out. But trust me, at this point, I was closer to fainting than jumping. What happens next? Well, it's a mix of bravery, stupidity, and a whole lot of gravity. Keep reading…

So, there I am, standing on the edge of doom, my legs shaking like they're auditioning for Strictly Come Dancing. I turn around to go back down, ready to save what little dignity I have left, when I spot them—kids. Loads of them, no older than four, shouting, "Come on, mister! Jump! Bloody jump!"

Now I'm not just scared—I'm absolutely mortified. These tiny humans, probably wearing armbands, are braver than me. And here I am, a grown man, frozen like a statue on top of a wobbly plank. I'm thinking, "This is it. I'm definitely going to die. Jackie's going to have to explain this to everyone: He died because a bunch of toddlers peer-pressured him off a diving board."

I turn back to face the pool, trying to summon the courage of a lion, but all I've got is the panic of a cat in a bathtub. And then—because this is me we're talking about—it happens. I slip. Of course, there's water on the diving board because why wouldn't there be? My foot goes flying, and before I know it, my bum slams down onto the board, and I spring off like I'm on a human-sized trampoline.

Now I'm in the air, flailing like a demented pigeon, when I somehow manage to do a full-on somersault. I hit the water with a smack so loud, I'm surprised it didn't set off car alarms in the parking lot. The pain? Oh, the pain. It felt like I belly-flopped into a brick wall. I'm convinced I've left an imprint of myself on the pool surface.

I get out of the water, limping, dripping, and clutching what's left of my dignity. Everyone around the pool is howling with laughter—kids, adults, the lifeguard, probably even Jackie. I can't hear a thing because the smack was so loud it left me deaf for two whole weeks. TWO WEEKS! I'm standing there thinking, I hope you're happy, Jackie. I've turned into the pool's comedy highlight of the year.

Lesson learned? If Jackie dares you to do something, don't just say no—run the other way, fast. Because otherwise, you'll end up half-deaf, embarrassed, and with a permanent fear of diving boards.

So, I'm limping over to Jackie after my death-defying leap of doom, dripping wet, bruised in places I didn't even know I had, and still hearing absolutely nothing because my ears are out of commission. And there she is, standing there cool as a cucumber, arms crossed, and with that look on her face.

As I get closer, she flashes me the biggest grin and says, "See? I told you that you could do it!"

I just stand there, blinking at her, thinking, Are you serious right now? I didn't "do it"—I accidentally launched myself into a mid-air circus act and smacked the water so hard I've lost my hearing and possibly part of my soul. But Jackie? Oh no, in her mind, I've just nailed an Olympic dive and proven her right.

She's practically glowing with pride, while I'm plotting revenge that involves her climbing that board next time. Only Jackie could watch me turn into a human cannonball and then act like it was all part of the plan!

Chapter 84: Standing Strong; Navigating Debt and Loss as a Single Parent of Five

Being a single parent to five kids is like being the captain of a pirate ship with a mutinous crew—except the treasure is just five minutes of peace, and you're constantly dodging metaphorical cannonballs. Toss in £60,000 of credit card debt, and suddenly it's not just the ship that's sinking. The annual interest alone was £20,000—a figure that made me briefly consider opening a lemonade stand or selling my soul (if only the market for that hadn't crashed).

Life had already thrown me the curveball of losing my beloved wife, shattering my world and leaving me to fill the roles of both mom and dad. Suddenly, I was the CEO of our household, responsible for not only food, clothing, and shelter but also hugs, bedtime stories, and pretending I understood algebra. Grief weighed on me like a heavy blanket, but I couldn't let it pin me down—my kids needed me. They were the reason I got out of bed every morning, even when I felt like crawling back under the covers and staying there for a decade.

The credit cards that once felt like life rafts during emergencies turned into anchors, dragging us deeper into a sea of debt. Each monthly statement was like a bad horror movie—one where the monster just kept getting bigger and scarier. Still, I couldn't afford to dwell on it. My kids weren't going to feed themselves, though they did offer helpful solutions like, "Can we have cereal for dinner?" (Answer: Yes, if it's on sale.)

There were nights when the house was quiet, and the weight of it all—grief, debt, responsibility—felt unbearable. I'd lie there, staring at the ceiling, playing a mental game of "What Can I Cut Next?" It was like financial Jenga, except pulling the wrong block could make everything collapse. Could I skip meals? (No, the kids would notice.) Sell the car? (No, the school drop-off line isn't bike-friendly.) Cancel the Wi-Fi? (Are you kidding? We'd have a mutiny.)

But amidst the chaos, something incredible happened: I found strength I didn't know I had. I became a master of survival, a black-belt budgeter, and the kind of resilient that only comes from realising your family has mistaken duct tape for a life hack instead of a red flag. The kids, bless them, were my motivation and my comic relief. When I was exhausted, they'd crack jokes or turn folding laundry into a competitive sport. (Spoiler: I always lose.)

Bit by bit, I chipped away at the mountain of debt. Each small victory felt monumental—like discovering a £10 note in your pocket, but multiplied by a thousand. The day I made my final credit card payment, I cried, laughed, and danced like a maniac in the kitchen. The kids thought I'd lost it, but I didn't care. For the first time in years, I felt free.

Looking back, those years were the toughest of my life, but also the most transformative. We didn't just survive; we grew stronger, together. The kids learned the value of perseverance, the importance of love, and how to find joy even when life felt like one long Monday morning. I learned that no matter how dark things get, there's always a spark of light if you're willing to look for it—or sometimes create it yourself, even if it means making shadow puppets during a power outage.

Today, we're on firmer ground. The debt is gone, the laughter is louder, and our bonds are unbreakable. Life isn't perfect, but it's ours—and that, more than anything, feels like the greatest treasure of all.

"There's more to this story, and I feel that the way its written captures it perfectly—the rest is something we'll keep to ourselves."

Chapter 85: The Hypnosis Horror Show; When the Unknown Speaks

This is a story that has to be told. I really didn't know where I should place this in the book, but trust me, this happened.

Why do things always happen to me? Well your about to find out.

If this story had been caught on video, I swear it would have gone viral—millions of views, no question. As you know, I'm a hypno-analyst, and one day, I was teaching a group of about fifteen eager students who wanted to learn the art of hypnosis. Everything was going smoothly until I got a panicked call from one of my students. She had been practicing an induction—a method of guiding someone into a trance—on one of her friends. Within ten seconds, her friend was out cold, deeply entranced, like a light had been switched off.

But then, something truly chilling happened. Slowly, her friend's head began to lift, almost as if pulled by an invisible string. Her eyes snapped open, but they weren't her eyes anymore. They were vacant, glassy, and dark, like a doll's eyes. Then, in the most bone-chilling voice—low, raspy, and echoing with something…inhuman—she croaked, "Help me…"

My student froze, paralyzed with fear. She had no idea what to do. The friend just sat there, staring blankly ahead, her head slightly tilted, still murmuring, "Help me." Desperately, my student managed to bring her out of the trance, but the experience left her shaken to the core. She called me in a panic, saying, "What should I do?"

I told her, "Bring her to the training. We'll hypnotise her in front of the class and see what happens." I mean, how could I not? This was a mystery too intriguing—and too unsettling—to ignore.

What could possibly go wrong? I have to stop tempting fate.

The day of the training came, and the air in the room was thick with anticipation. The friend sat in the chair, looking completely normal, even a little nervous. I reassured her, guided her into a trance, and at first, everything seemed fine. But then... It began.

Her head lifted again, just like my student had described, as if something unseen was pulling her upward. Her eyes snapped open, lifeless and glassy, staring straight through me. The room went cold—I mean freezing, like the temperature had dropped twenty degrees in an instant.

Her head lifted so slowly it was almost unbearable to watch, like something out of a nightmare. Her eyes locked onto mine, and for a moment, it felt as though she was looking straight into my soul, pulling at something deep inside me that I didn't even know was there. A chill ran down my spine. The room seemed to darken, and the air grew thick.

Then, ever so slowly, she tilted her head to the side, her movements unnervingly deliberate, almost mechanical. Her gaze shifted from me to the person sitting next to her—a young woman named Michaela. For a split second, Michaela froze, her face pale and wide-eyed. And then, as if an invisible hand had pushed her, she jumped out of her seat, letting out a sharp gasp, and dashed to the other side of the room like her life depended on it.

Someone muttered, "This wasn't in the syllabus."

No kidding, genius.

The class erupted into chaos. Some gasped, others screamed softly, and a few just sat there, clutching their seats as if they couldn't believe what they were seeing. Michaela, now pressed against the wall, stammered, "What... what was that?" Her voice shook as if she'd just seen a ghost—or something worse.

I turned back to the woman in the trance, her head still tilted, and her eyes still eerily vacant. She hadn't moved a muscle, but her presence felt heavier, darker, like the entire room was caught in her gravity

I took a deep breath, steadied myself, and said firmly, "I don't want to speak to you—I want to speak to Sharon."

For a moment, the room felt like it held its breath. And then, just as suddenly as it had appeared, that other presence seemed to recede. Sharon's voice came through, soft, shaky, and confused. "What's going on?" she asked, as if she'd just woken up from a strange dream. It was such a surreal moment, hearing her speak so naturally after everything we'd just witnessed.

I looked her in the eye and asked, "Do you want to carry on?" Without hesitation, she replied, "Yes." Brave, I thought, maybe too brave. Within a second, her head dropped, her body slackened, and she was back under, just as deeply entranced as before.

This time, I didn't waste any time. With a voice that I hoped sounded authoritative, I said, "This is not your body. You have to leave."

I have to be honest with you—I had absolutely no idea what the hell I was doing. I wasn't following any textbook technique or strategy. It was like the words were coming from somewhere deep inside me, instinctual, primal. But as soon as I said them, I felt a shift in the air, as if I'd struck a nerve.

The head slowly lifted again, and this time, the look she gave me froze the blood in my veins. Her eyes—Sharon's eyes—were filled with something alien, something cold, and calculating. There was no fear, no hesitation, just an unyielding defiance. It was clear—she wasn't going anywhere.

The tension in the room was suffocating. My heart was pounding, but I didn't dare break eye contact. "You have to leave," I repeated, trying to channel whatever force had helped me find the words before. But the thing inside her just stared at me, unwavering, almost mocking.

In that moment, I realized I wasn't just dealing with a trance—I was facing something far more stubborn, far more...other. And Sharon, poor Sharon, was caught in the middle.

I knew I had to do what I do best—I had to connect, not just with words but with feelings and empathy. This wasn't about following any script or method; it was about reaching out from the heart, speaking not just to what was happening but to whoever—or whatever—this presence was.

I asked, gently but firmly, "Who are you? Why won't you leave?"

For a moment, there was silence, heavy and tense. But then I felt a shift, something subtle but undeniable. It was as if the energy in the room began to change. Slowly, the figure started to soften, the defiance in its expression fading. He seemed to sense what I was doing—my intent, my openness—and it was like a wall began to come down. For the first time, he smiled, faint and hesitant, but unmistakably a smile.

As I continued to talk to him, a story began to unfold. He told me—through fragmented words and emotions—that he lived in the 11th century, a boy of just 14 years. He had suffered deeply in his short life. His father was cruel, and he hated him with a passion, but his mother—oh, how he loved her. She was his world, his only light. He struggled to speak, his words halting and broken, and then it became clear why: his tongue had been cut out. The pain of his past, the resentment, and the isolation radiated from him.

I asked him how he came to be here, with Sharon. He explained, in his way, that he had found her when she was just 3, a vulnerable, lost girl. Something about her called to him—a kindred spirit in her pain. He entered her life then, not to harm her, but almost as if seeking refuge. Over time, he became a part of her, woven into her being, like a shadow that had been there so long it felt natural.

It was heart-breaking and profound. I could feel his pain, his longing for connection, and even his strange sense of protectiveness toward Sharon. This wasn't just an entity to expel—it was a boy who had been trapped, lost in time and in his own sorrow. And in that moment, I knew what I had to do next

His name was Richard. The moment he told me, something shifted—it felt as though the room itself softened, like his name brought with it a piece of his humanity that had been lost for so long. I looked into his eyes, and I spoke gently but with purpose.

"You know, Richard, you can't stay here. This isn't your place anymore. Your mother...she's been waiting for you. She's missed you so much. She's still out there, waiting for you, ready to welcome you with open arms."

I could see his expression change, the defiance completely gone now. A look of longing crossed his face, as though the mention of his mother had awakened something deep within him. I leaned in, speaking straight from my heart, "You could both have another life, Richard. A better life. You don't have to stay trapped here, clinging to what was. I know it's hard, but I can help you. Would you like me to help you?"

For a moment, the room was still, and then, slowly, Richard nodded. A faint, almost childlike smile crept across his face. It was the kind of smile that carried both relief and hope—a smile spoke softly, but with conviction, as I prepared him for what was about to happen. "Richard, in a moment, the angels will come down. They'll wrap you in a blanket of light and take you to your mother. She's waiting for you, Richard. This is your time. Say goodbye to Sharon now."

For a brief moment, he hesitated, as if holding on to the only life he'd known for centuries. But then, he turned his gaze inward, his expression softening. "Goodbye, Sharon," he whispered, his voice tinged with both sadness and gratitude.

And then it happened. In that instant, Richard left Sharon's body. Her entire body jolted, as if a sudden force had passed through her. It wasn't a slight twitch or a tremor—it was a full, unexpected jump, and for a heart-stopping moment, I thought bloody hell she's dead. Panic surged through me as I stared at her motionless form.

My first thought? Oh no. That's it. She's gone. I've just killed someone with hypnosis.

Cue my internal meltdown: Do I call an ambulance? A priest? My lawyer? Can I even have a lawyer after this?

Meanwhile, Sharon's motionless form just lay there, looking like she'd hit the reset button on her entire operating system. My students were no help—they all looked equally horrified, except for one guy in the back who appeared to be praying under his breath. I half-expected him to start sprinkling holy water from his water bottle.

But then, I saw it—her chest rising and falling, slow and steady. She was breathing. Relief flooded over me like a tidal wave. Sharon was okay.

Relief hit me so hard I almost needed CPR myself.

It was as if a weight had been lifted from the room. The energy that had felt so dark, so heavy, was gone, replaced with a lightness I couldn't describe. I looked at Sharon's peaceful face, her body completely relaxed, and I knew—Richard was finally at peace.

We gently brought Sharon out of the trance, and the first thing she said was that she felt lighter, as though a heavy burden she hadn't even known she was carrying had finally been lifted. Something had shifted, deeply and profoundly. Did I mention that Sharon had been possessed once before, when she was younger? At that time, religion had helped her find relief. But this time, the process was different, more personal—and it seemed to truly set her free.

When Sharon left, she looked like a new person, as though a part of her soul had been restored. Later, I spoke to the students about what had just happened. Many of them admitted that their hairs had been standing on end the entire time. They said it felt like being in the middle of a horror movie—except this was real, and they'd witnessed it with their own eyes.

Sharon's life transformed after that day. She found love, met someone wonderful, and the last I heard, she's living happily in Texas. It's remarkable how things turned around for her, how that moment of release opened up a whole new chapter. Seeing her happiness now makes everything we went through that day feel worth it. It's a reminder of just how powerful and life-changing these experiences can be.

Chapter 86: The Day I Nearly Flew Off a 4-Story Roof; A True Dockside Disaster

Let me take you back to when I was about 20, working for my Uncle Wolfy—yes, Uncle Wolfy, a man who, I swear, operated on vibes and sheer luck. This day? It was one for the books. We were down by the docks, working on these ancient buildings overlooking the River Mersey. These things were over 250 years old, practically crumbling relics, and for reasons I'll never understand, we were up on the roof.

Now, when I say "roof," I don't mean a cute little bungalow roof. No, this was four stories high, towering over the docks like something out of a Dickensian nightmare. And the best part? No harnesses, no safety gear—just me, my questionable footwear, and a prayer. To this day, I have no clue what the bloody hell we were doing up there. Something with the chimney? Knocking off lead? Who knows! All I know is, I was one wrong move away from starring in my own obituary.

The roof was slick from rain, and for some inexplicable reason, I was wearing pumps. Yes, pumps.

Not boots, not trainers—pumps, because apparently, I wanted to maximize my chances of plummeting into the River Mersey. Every step felt like I was ice skating on the edge of disaster.

At one point, I lost my footing. My heart stopped. One leg slid out from under me, and I swear I saw my life flash before my eyes. I was halfway convinced I'd end up somersaulting into the river or landing in some poor Docker's fish and chips. If the fire brigade had been there with a safety net, I'd have dived into it just for the drama.

Holding onto the chimney for dear life while Uncle Wolfy carried on like this was a perfectly normal day. Suddenly, one of the chimney bricks came loose in my hand. The roof, wet and slippery, turned into my personal death slide. I started sliding down, claws out, and my nails scraping against the slates like some kind of desperate, terrified cat. My mind went blank except for one screaming thought: This is it. This is how I die

As I slid closer to the edge, I glanced down. Big mistake. The drop was about 300 feet, straight down onto cold, unforgiving concrete. No water, no soft landing, just a splashy red ending. I clawed harder, praying for some kind of miracle. Then, BANG. My saviour: a cast iron gutter. It caught me right at the edge and stopped my slide. I can't explain the relief.

When I finally got off that roof (with all my limbs intact, miraculously), I needed a therapist, a stiff drink, and possibly a medal for surviving.

I was done. Shaking, sweating, and swearing off roofs for life. My Uncle Wolfy? He just looked at me, laughed, and said, "You made it! Now, stop messing about and grab the tools." The nerve of the man.

That day taught me one thing: if someone ever invites you to work on a roof with no safety gear in the rain, just say no. Or at least wear better shoes. Or better still, run like bloody hell.

Chapter 87: From Fresh to Frantic: The Day I Accidentally Bathed in Vim

When I was 14, I experienced what can only be described as The Great Bath-Time Debacle. There I was, all innocent and carefree, ready to powder myself up with some nice, luxurious talc. I reached for the container, eyes closed, and confidently started slapping it on like I was in a glamorous deodorant commercial.

Except... it wasn't talc.

It was Vim. Yes, the cleaning powder. BLEACHING powder. Within seconds, I noticed something was off. First, the smell—why did I smell like a freshly disinfected kitchen? Then the texture—this wasn't silky talc; this was... sandpaper from hell!

The realization hit me like a truck. I opened my eyes (big mistake) and saw the container. My brain froze. "VIM?! WHY AM I BATHING IN CLEANING POWDER?!" Cue absolute chaos. I turned the shower into a panic-wash station, scrubbing like I was being prepped for surgery. My inner monologue was screaming, "Is my skin going to bleach? Am I going to turn into a walking kitchen counter? Will my parents notice I smell like the bathroom sink?!"

The worst part? I was convinced I'd accidentally invented human dishwashing. My skin squeaked—actually squeaked. I was like a freshly waxed car. And my eyes? Thankfully, they were shut the whole time, but I still flushed them like I was in an emergency lab demo, just in case.

In the end, I survived, but my dignity didn't. Lesson learned: don't just read the label—triple-check it. Otherwise, you might end up as the human embodiment of Mr. Clean.

Chapter 88: The gas leak with the darts

The gas leak with the darts… oh man, this one really could have been the end of me. Picture this: I'm eight years old, at my auntie's house one summer. My cousin Graham and I are in the garage, bored out of our tiny little minds, when we stumble across a set of darts. Obviously, this screams opportunity. Graham, being the mastermind of our duo, points to a brush pole and goes, "Bet you can't hit that."

Challenge accepted. First throw? Bulls-eye. The dart lands dead centre, and Graham's jaw drops. But he's not about to let me off easy. "Bet you can't do it again," he says. Oh, now it's on. Second throw? Whack. Nailed it, like I've been training for this my whole life. At this point, I'm feeling unstoppable—like the Michael Jordan of darts. Naturally, I go, "I could do this blindfolded!" Because, you know, when you're eight and full of yourself, logic doesn't stand a chance.

So I throw the dart, blindfolded, and. It goes straight into a lead gas pipe. And when I say gas started spewing out, I mean SPEWING. The pipe was hissing like it was auditioning for a horror movie. The hissing sound is deafening. Graham and I are frozen, just staring at it like two deer caught in the headlights of our own stupidity.

Then it hits me: gas... sparks... KABOOM. My brilliant eight-year-old brain comes up with the perfect plan. I turn to Graham and go, "Don't tell anyone." Yep. Gas is spewing out, the whole garage smells like doom, and my grand solution is silence. Genius.

But thankfully, Graham had a slightly better survival instinct. He ran to get his dad. Meanwhile, I'm standing there, trying to mentally prepare for the explosion and the scolding of a lifetime. His dad walks in, takes one look at the gas pipe we've created, and—get this—grabs a bar of soap. A bar of soap. Cool as anything, he slathers it over the hole like he's frosting a cake, and just like that, the gas leak is sealed. No panic, no shouting—just soap and problem solved.

I'm standing there, sweating like I just ran a marathon, waiting for him to blow up at me (figuratively this time). But nope. All he says is, "That'll hold until we get it fixed." That's it. No yelling. No grounding.

Nothing. I'm still trying to figure out how soap just saved my life—and my reputation.

Now, every time I see a dartboard, I'm reminded of the day I almost turned my auntie's house into a crater... and how a bar of soap was the real MVP. Lesson learned: if you ever think about playing darts near a gas pipe? Don't. But if you do, make sure there's a calm adult nearby—and maybe a bar of soap, just in case.

Chapter 89: The Golf Swing That Took Out My Cousin; A Lesson in Keeping Your Distance

The golf swing with my cousin getting knocked out... oh boy, here we go again. So, there I was, back at it with my cousin Graham. For some reason, we always managed to turn innocent fun into absolute chaos. This time, it was a golf club. What could possibly go wrong, right? (I really need to stop saying that.)

Anyway, I was really into golf at the time—practicing my swing like I was prepping for the Masters. Graham, curious as ever, was watching me. "Do that swing again," he says. So, I line up, channel my inner pro, and give it my best shot. He's impressed, of course. But then he gets really close. Like, dangerously close. "One more time!" he says, practically leaning into my backswing.

Well, me being the accommodating cousin, I oblige. I go for another big swing, and—WHACK. The club connects... but not with the golf ball. Nope. It connects right with Graham's head. One second he's standing there, all excited, and the next? Boom. Flat on the ground. Unconscious.

I look down at him, frozen. "Not again…" I mutter to myself. Of course, it had to be me. It's always me. He's out cold, and I'm standing there, holding the club like some kind of criminal caught red-handed.

Thankfully, he eventually came to—probably with the world's worst headache—and, shockingly, didn't seem to hate me for it. But to this day, every time I pick up a golf club, I think about that swing… and how Graham was the ball that day. Lesson learned: never stand too close to someone practicing their golf swing—especially if that someone is me.

Chapter 90: Well, Here We Go Again; My Journey into Fitness Hell

So, there I was, fresh off a heart attack, thinking, "You know what? Time to heal, time to get back to the gym." Logical, right? But little did I know, healing would involve being tortured by Simon, a fitness instructor who's less "personal trainer" and more "alien warrior in disguise."

Let me paint you a picture of Simon. Lovely guy, great smile, absolutely bonkers. This man has a death wish—or maybe he's just not human. Who cycles 70 miles, runs 20, and swims 10 miles in one go? That's not fitness; that's a cry for help. And somehow, I thought it was a good idea to let him push me to my limit.

We're talking hour-long sessions, twice a week—otherwise known as my personal ticket to the fiery pits of fitness hell. Every session, Simon ups the ante. Today? He's got me chucking 12-kilogram balls at the ground like I'm trying to smash my way to China. And not just once—four sets of 12. Then there's the benching: two 25-kilogram weights while lying flat on the floor, no cheating allowed. Trust me, I've tried. He's got a sixth sense for laziness. I keep telling him I hate him, and you know what he does? Smiles. Smiles like a man who thrives on my misery.

And don't get me started on the ropes. You know, those heavy, God-forsaken ropes you whip up and down with your arms? Yeah, those. He's got me swinging them like I'm trying to summon a storm. Oh, and by the way, I'm 71. That's right, seventy-one years old. But Simon? I'm convinced he thinks I'm 17. Maybe Specsavers should sponsor him.

But here's the weird thing: I actually love that he pushes me this hard. Don't get me wrong—I'll complain, grumble, and question my life choices the entire session. But deep down, I wouldn't have it any other way. Simon is genuinely one of the most wonderful, inspiring people I've ever met.

To mix things up, we've decided to set up a chess game. Apparently, Simon's into chess. Well, I have to beat him at something, don't I? But honestly, given his superhuman streak, I'm not feeling too confident. He'll probably end up checkmating me while doing one-armed push-ups.

Oh, but wait—there's more! Simon's latest invention? Pull-ups. Not just regular pull-ups (because apparently, those are too "easy" for me at 71)—no, I'm doing pull-ups with a weighted vest. A weighted bloody vest. Because, clearly, gravity alone wasn't already my mortal enemy.

And it doesn't stop there. It's not just one set, oh no. Its four sets of seven, and just when I think I've survived, Simon casually decides to increase the weight. Whenever he feels like it. No warning, no discussion—just, "Here, have an extra couple of kilos. You're welcome."

At this point, I'm seriously questioning my sanity. Is Simon insane? Am I insane? Or is this just some weird fever dream I haven't woken up from? Honestly, it's probably me. After all, I'm the one showing up to these sessions like some sort of masochistic glutton for punishment.

But here's the thing: deep down, I know I wouldn't trade it for the world. (Though I might trade it for a doughnut and a lie-down.)

Honestly, if I survive Simon's boot camp from outer space, I'm either going to be ripped or I'm going to haunt him as the fittest ghost in history.

So, if you've got a death wish—or just want to find out what it feels like to cry while doing push-ups—I'm leaving Simon's email at the back of this book. Why? Because if I'm being dragged through the fiery pits of fitness hell, I'm not going alone. Misery loves company, and trust me, Simon will make you very miserable.

Think of it as a group bonding experience! We'll laugh (barely), cry (a lot), and question our life choices together. So, go ahead, sign up. I dare you. Let's all suffer under Simon's reign of terror and call it "self-improvement." You're welcome.

Either way, it'll be the workout journey of your life.

Oh, did I mention I roped my two daughters, Shanna and Gema, into this madness? Yep, now Simon is their fitness instructor too. I figured, if I'm having all this "fun," why should I keep it to myself? Sharing is caring, right?

The weirdest part? They actually love it. Can you believe that? They come out of their sessions grinning like lunatics while I'm hobbling out looking like I've just survived a battlefield. "Isn't Simon amazing?" they gush, while I'm over here plotting how to superglue his dumbbells to the floor.

Honestly, I don't know what's stranger: the fact that they're enjoying it or the fact that Simon somehow hasn't scared them off yet. Either way, I guess it's a family bonding experience… even if it's through mutual suffering.

Chapter 91: Kora; The Angel Who Saved Zak

This is a story close to my heart—about how my son, Zak, met Kora. It all began with a special holiday, a gift for my 70th birthday. A trip to Israel, 14 nights, and oh, what a journey it turned out to be.

We started in Modiin, staying with family—David and Elaine. They immigrated to Israel 50 years ago, and it was such a joy to reconnect. Jackie, first cousin, felt like the sister I never had—my older sister. We spent a week there, catching up, reminiscing, and just soaking in the warmth of family. It was wonderful. Truly wonderful.

Then, we moved on to Tel Aviv. And that's where the magic happened.

You see, Kora came into Zak's life in a way that felt almost... divinely orchestrated. Like she was meant to be there. And not just for Zak—no, for me too. She brought something special into our lives, something I can't quite explain.

Kora wasn't just a person; she felt like an angel. You're about to find out why. Around the 10th day of our trip, I wasn't feeling too good. The excitement and energy I'd carried through the first part of the holiday started to wane. All I could think about was home—how much I just wanted to be there, in my own space, surrounded by familiar comforts. I even started wondering if maybe the trip had been too much for me.

But little did I know, this was the moment when everything was about to change. Something extraordinary was about to happen that would lift my spirits and make me see this trip in an entirely different light.

It wasn't just about me anymore—it was about Zak. And Kora. This is where their story truly begins.

So there we were, Zak and I, spending the day at the beach in Tel Aviv. I wasn't feeling my best, but the sea air and the sound of the waves were comforting. I stayed on the beach, soaking it all in, while Zak, as he often does, wandered off to do his own thing.

It was then that he started chatting with this girl. A simple conversation, the kind you'd never think much of at the moment. But little did Zak know, this encounter would change his life forever.

Just a week before this trip, Zak and I had a conversation. He told me he was planning to come back to Israel in October—for three months, no less. I wasn't too keen on the idea, I'll admit. It felt impulsive, like one of Zak's adventurous plans. But Zak is Zak; he always has a plan. What he didn't know, though, was that this plan wasn't really his. It was life's plan—or maybe something bigger. And that plan had a name: Kora.

When we returned home from Israel, I noticed something had shifted. Zak couldn't stop chatting with Kora. They were texting, calling—every moment they had, they were connecting. It was as though their meeting on that beach had unlocked something in both of them, something that was meant to be.

And just like that, what started as a casual holiday became the beginning of a story that none of us saw coming.

She's from Poland, and over the months that followed their meeting, she and Zak built a life that spanned between Liverpool and Poland. They'd travel back and forth—she'd stay here, and Zak would spend time in Poland. Slowly but surely, their connection deepened. What started as a chance meeting on a beach in Tel Aviv transformed into something unshakable.

Remember when I said she was like an angel sent to Zak? Let me tell you why.

In October, tragedy struck Israel. The country was attacked—kibbutzim were invaded, and innocent men, women, and children were brutally slaughtered by Hamas terrorists. Over 1,200 people lost their lives, and 250 were taken hostage. It was a horrifying, unimaginable day.

Now here's where the gravity of it all hits me. If Zak hadn't been with me in Israel that day in May... if he hadn't met Kora... if their lives hadn't collided in that perfect, fateful moment... he might have been there. Zak, my adventurous, fearless son, might have been in Israel on that day in October.

I know him so well. He would have been drawn to the idea of staying on a kibbutz, to immersing himself in the culture, to living that life. It's exactly the kind of thing Zak would do, and my heart shudders to think of what might have happened.

But he wasn't there. He wasn't anywhere near that horror. He was with Kora, safe in Poland, where life had gently steered him. And I know in my heart—it was her. She was his guardian. His angel. She saved him, just by being who she is, just by existing in his life.

Sometimes the universe moves in ways we can't comprehend, in ways that feel almost supernatural. Kora wasn't just a chance encounter on a beach. She was the reason Zak was where he needed to be—safe, loved, and far from the darkness that swept across Israel.

And for that, I will always, always believe in the magic of that day when they met. Kora wasn't just sent to Zak. She was sent to us all.

Let me tell you a little about Kora— this extraordinary, quirky woman who somehow managed to charm Zak—and, to be honest, the rest of us too. She's one of those people who makes life endlessly interesting in the best, most unpredictable ways. But here's the thing: she hides eggs.

Yes, eggs. Like, actual eggs. Who does that? I'm not kidding—she tucks them away in the strangest places. The fridge? Sure, that's normal. But the cupboard? Behind the toaster? In a coat pocket? Really? When Zak first told me about it, I thought he was pulling my leg. Why on earth would anyone hide eggs? Are they part of some secret operation? Is she planning an egg-themed scavenger hunt?

It's one of those delightfully absurd quirks that just makes you laugh—and, oddly enough, makes you love her even more. She has this way of making even the simplest things feel magical or hilarious, like life is one big adventure full of surprises.

She's the kind of person who lights up a room without even trying, who makes you feel like the little oddities in life are worth celebrating. And honestly, that's exactly what Zak needed—someone so vibrant, unexpected, and unapologetically unique.

Because when you think about it, who wouldn't want someone in their life who hides eggs?

She reminds me so much of, Rudi, Shanna, Gema, Josh, and Zak —those rare, special people who seem to carry the sun within them. The kind who walk into a room and instantly make it brighter, filling the space with warmth, laughter, and light. Just being around them, you feel the world become a little softer, a little kinder, as if the sun itself decided to shine a little brighter for everyone in their presence. Kora has that same magic about her, the kind that can turn an ordinary day into something unforgettable

Chapter 92: How I Swapped a Car That Wasn't Even Mine to Save a Holiday

Oh, buckle up because this is where the story takes a very creative turn. Picture this: seven days before the holiday of a lifetime in the sunny south of France, Jackie and I are buzzing with excitement. Except, as usual, I'm about as organized as a cat in a laser tag arena. Planning is for boring people, right? We're "wing-it" experts!

Now, the cast of this soon-to-be blockbuster adventure includes Jackie, Rudi, Shanna, Gema, Joshi, Zak, and yours truly—basically, enough people to field a decent football team and still have a sub. The issue? Our car is as practical as a pair of flip-flops in the snow. Seven people plus luggage? We tried. Oh, we tried. It was less "family road trip" and more "clown car at a circus." The wheels practically disappeared under the weight, and the poor suspension was weeping.

Enter the genius idea: let's get a Serena 8-seater! Problem solved, right? Wrong. Our credit was so bad that the finance company laughed us out of the room. I think they actually sent a sympathy card afterward. And who gets the blame? Me. Apparently, it's my fault. And yeah, okay, it probably was my fault, but details, details.

So now I've got to come up with a plan. And here's where things get... inventive.

So here we are, six days now before we're supposed to be off on this epic holiday, and it's all about to implode. The finance company gives us a lifeline: Find a guarantor. Translation? Find someone willing to bet their sanity (and wallet) on us never missing a payment. If we don't pay, they're on the hook. Simple enough, right? Wrong. Because, really, who in their right mind would sign their name to five years of potential chaos for a caravan holiday? Exactly.

But hey, I'm a man on a mission. Sleeping in a car for eternity isn't on my bucket list. Enter: my neighbour, who lives next door to Jackie's mum and dad. Lovely bloke, nice enough, and, crucially, just gullible enough to listen to me. So, armed with a smile and the most convincing sales pitch of my life, I march over there, paperwork in hand. I paint a picture so rosy it would make a travel agent jealous—promising him we'd never miss a single payment, not even if the apocalypse rolled around. Miraculously, he says yes! I'm halfway to a victory lap.

But hold on—there's one more signature needed. No problem, right? WRONG. The next day, I go back to seal the deal, and the man does a complete U-turn. "Nope," he says. "I've been thinking about it, and I'm not doing it." Excuse me, WHAT? Four days to go, and now my entire holiday (and probably my relationship) is dangling by a thread. Jackie is sharpening her knives, preparing to turn me into a cautionary tale.

But I'm not giving up. Oh no. Desperate times call for desperate measures, and here's where my genius—or insanity—kicks in.

I go full charm offensive. I show up at his house with his favourite snacks and a bottle of wine like it was date night. I tell him I've been thinking about how amazing it would be to show him real gratitude. "You're a hero," I say, laying it on thick. He's wavering, but not quite there yet. So, I pull out the big guns.

I offer to do his gardening. For a YEAR. Yes, you heard me. A YEAR of mowing his lawn, trimming his hedges, and probably battling the local wasp population. I promise to walk his dog, help him with shopping, whatever it takes. At this point, I'm basically offering to become his unpaid butler.

So, we're now four days away from this supposed dream holiday, but at this rate, the only dream I'm having is one where I'm curled up in a car park, living out of a glove compartment. The neighbour—my last hope for salvation—has gone from "Yes, I'll sign," to "Not a chance." Jackie's already looking up DIY coffin kits, probably for me, and I'm spiralling into a black hole of panic.

Then, in my moment of sheer desperation, an idea hits me. A ridiculous idea. A this-will-probably-haunt-me-forever idea. I decide to bribe him. Not with a bottle of wine, not with a heartfelt plea, but with a car. That's right, a whole bloody car. Genius? Maybe. Stupid? Oh, definitely.

Now here's the thing: the car I'm offering isn't exactly mine. Well, technically, it is mine, but only in the "let's not get into the nitty-gritty of ownership" sense. The kind of ownership where the paperwork's still questionable and the car's not even fully paid off yet. But hey, desperate times, right?

I march over to his house, keys in hand, and lay it all out. "Look," I say, "I know you're worried about being a guarantor, but what if I sweeten the deal?" He raises an eyebrow. I dangle the keys in front of him like they're Willy Wonka's golden ticket. "This baby could be yours. £1,500 worth of glorious wheels. Just sign the paper, and the car is yours."

He stares at me, stunned. Probably trying to figure out if I've lost my mind. (I have) "Are you serious?" he asks. I nod so hard I nearly dislocate something. "Absolutely. A car for your signature. That's the deal."

And guess what? He actually says yes. The man signs his name on the dotted line, and I hand over the keys. As he admires his shiny new bribe, I'm celebrating like I just won the lottery. Sure, I've lost a car I didn't technically have the right to give away, but who cares? The holiday is ON.

Jackie doesn't know the full story yet. (And if she does find out, pray for me.) But as far as I'm concerned, I've just pulled off the deal of the century. Sure, I've sold a car that wasn't fully mine, but hey, that's a problem for Future Me.

And thus, with a neighbour-turned-guarantor and a slightly questionable vehicle exchange, we're finally ready to head to the south of France. What could possibly go wrong from here?

...Stay tuned.

Chapter 93: Stuck in the Door Disaster

These are the last two stories of the book, and trust me, they had to be told. It's the kind of stories that's only funny once the trauma wears off—so, about five minutes after it happened.

Picture this: I'm out knocking on doors for British Gas, just trying to earn an honest living, when my two boys, Josh and Zak, both 13, decide to rewrite the manual on bad decisions. Somehow, they've managed to lose the front door key. How? Don't ask—I gave up questioning these things years ago.

The boys get home from school, realize they're locked out, and instead of waiting patiently for me, they decide to get innovative. They wander round to the back of the house and spot the old Georgian door.

Now, this door has a broken glass pane at the bottom—ten inches by ten inches. Barely big enough for a housecat, let alone a fully-grown, overconfident teenage boy.

Josh, the mastermind, looks at Zak and goes, "You're small—you can get through that!" And for some unfathomable reason, Zak agrees.

So, there's Zak, head-first through this tiny glass pane. He manages to squeeze his head in, then his shoulders, then his arms. He's halfway through, probably thinking he's a genius; until physics intervenes. The boy gets stuck. Properly stuck. His upper body is inside the house, his legs and bum are flailing around outside like he's training for the Olympic swim team.

Josh, helpful as ever, immediately starts screaming with laughter. "Dad's gonna kill us!" he shouts, between hysterics. Zak, meanwhile, is yelling from the other side of the door: "I'M STUCK! JOSH, GET ME OUT!"

At this point, Josh does the most logical thing; he calls me. I'm miles away, mid-shift, when the phone rings.

"Dad! Dad, Zak's stuck in the door!"

"What do you mean, stuck?!" I shout, already sweating through my British Gas uniform.

"He tried to climb through the glass, and now he's stuck! His bum is sticking out the door!"

"What?! Is he hurt?"

"No, but…" click. The phone goes dead.

Can you imagine the scene I'm picturing? My child, half-inside, half-outside, like some kind of bizarre human sandwich board. I'm panicking; do I call the fire brigade? The police? Is there a special unit for idiot extraction?

I drove home at warp speed, fully expecting to find Zak still wedged in the door, Josh live-streaming it on YouTube, and half the street gathered with popcorn.

But when I finally get there, Zak is free. How he got out? I have no idea. Maybe he shimmied, maybe the house gave up and let him in out of pity. All I know is, the Georgian door is wrecked, Zak is scratched up and sulking, and Josh is grinning like the Cheshire Cat.

"Are you okay?!" I ask, out of breath.

Zak just glares at me. "I don't want to talk about it."

Josh, still laughing, pipes up: "Dad, he looked like Winnie the Pooh when he got stuck in Rabbit's house!"

And honestly? I couldn't even be mad. The visual of Zak wedged in that door—arms flailing, bum sticking out—is burned into my brain forever. I should've been furious about the door, the scratches, the chaos... but all I could do was laugh.

Moral of the story? Never lose your key. And if you do, don't let Josh take charge.

Chapter 94: The Day the Key Disappeared: A Christmas Comedy of Errors

So, it's near Christmas, freezing cold—the kind of cold where your breath freezes mid-air and your nose goes numb just thinking about going outside. Shanna's on a school trip. Gema's on a school trip. Neither will be back until 6:00 PM. Perfect, right? Except, before Gema leaves, she decides she needs the front door key.

"Why?" I ask.

"Just to grab something from the house," she says casually, like this isn't going to spiral into disaster.

Here's the thing: we've only got one key. One bloody key. Why? I don't know, but it's like we were living in some survival show: 'Who Can Function With the Fewest House Keys?'

I look Gema in the eye and say, "Don't go to school yet. Wait for me. I just need to take the twins to school,

I won't be long. Wait for me, Gema! I need to get back in the house."

Off I go. I take the twins, who were six at the time, to school, probably arguing over who looked at who wrong or whose gloves smelled the worst. I get back, and guess what? Gema's gone.

She's gone. With the key.

"You have GOT to be kidding me," I mutter, standing there in the freezing cold like some abandoned extra in a sad Christmas movie.

Now I'm locked out of my own house, I've got clients coming all day (because, trust me, I didn't just have one job—I had about ten), and no way to get in. So what do I do? I go full detective mode.

Check my pockets: empty.

Check the car: nothing.

Check the garage, because why not? Still nothing.

Down the drain. At this point, I'm half-expecting a rat to toss the key back at me.

Then I start calling anyone and everyone who might have a spare key. Friends, neighbours, random distant relatives—everyone's away until later. Of course they are. Everyone's mysteriously "not home."

And so, there I am: keyless, cold, and raging. I'm muttering to myself like a lunatic, "Gema's in BIG trouble. Big. Trouble."

Then I decide, you know what? It's near Christmas—let's try to salvage the day. I'll go Christmas shopping, pick the twins up at 3 o'clock, take them for something to eat, and just... wait until 6:00 PM when Gema gets home.

Well 6:00 PM arrives. Like clockwork, the house fills up—Shanna's home, Gema's home, everyone's back. Finally, we can get in the house.

And there's Gema, sitting there like a little angel who's done nothing wrong.

I turn to her and unleash: "GEMA, I TOLD YOU TO WAIT FOR ME THIS MORNING! WHY DID YOU LEAVE WITH THE KEY?"

Gema, completely calm, looks me dead in the eye and says, "I did give you the key."

"No, you didn't!"

"Yes, I did."

"No. You. Did. Not."

We're going back and forth now like it's a courtroom drama. I'm practically pacing. Then, out of pure frustration, I shove my hands in my pockets—probably for warmth—and that's when it happens.

The key. The bloody key.

It drops into my hand like it's been teleported there by a team of elves. I stare at it, stunned, like I've just pulled Excalibur from a stone.

You know when something so ridiculous happens that you start questioning your entire life? That was me.

I stood there, mouth open, frozen in disbelief. That key was not in my pocket this morning. It couldn't have been. It was like the universe spent all day winding me up for its own entertainment.

And there's Gema, smirking like the cat who got the cream. "Told you I gave it to you."

At that point, I was so defeated I couldn't even argue. I just sat down, holding the key like it was mocking me.

Moral of the story? Always have a spare key. And if you think you're losing your mind, don't worry—your kids will make sure you do.

Chapter 95: The Heart That Brought Us Closer; A Story of Love and Gratitude

When I had the heart attack, I need to tell you about the incredible people who stood by me—my beautiful family and our amazing friends. But let me make something very clear: they're not just friends; they are family.

They showed me a love so pure, so selfless, that it will stay with me for the rest of my life. I will never forget their kindness, their presence, their unwavering support.

Every single day, they were there—helping, sitting with me in my bedroom, watching TV, eating, drinking, and laughing. Just being there. They kept me going when I didn't think I could keep going myself.

Caroline—oh, Caroline—my beautiful friend with the kindest, most golden heart, even though she drives me absolutely crazy sometimes! Steph, who has such a beautiful nature which shines so brightly.

Hareesh and Varsha, two of the most beautiful souls I've ever had the privilege of knowing. I was so honoured to watch them get married in Singapore, to be a part of their incredible journey together. And then, of course, my beautiful family—my heart, my soul, my everything.

You are all my reason for living. You are my strength, my joy, my life. Words could never be enough to express what you mean to me. Thank you, from the deepest corners of my heart, for being there. Always."

Chapter 96: A New Chapter; The Endless Journey of Life

When I stop and look back at my life, I'm struck by the sheer magnitude of it all. What a breath-taking, awe-inspiring journey it has been! Each moment, every heartbeat, has been part of a story so rich, so alive, that it fills me with gratitude and wonder. I've climbed mountains of joy, weathered storms of sorrow, and walked paths I never could have predicted. Each step, whether triumphant or painful, has carved meaning into my soul.

But this isn't the end—not even close. Life is far too infinite for that. It doesn't end; it transforms, flowing from one chapter into the next like an unstoppable river. And now, as one chapter draws to a close, I feel the thrill of what's to come. This isn't just the turning of a page; it's the opening of a brand-new book, alive with possibilities and brimming with hope.

The beauty of life is its relentless capacity for renewal. It gives us second chances, fresh starts, and endless opportunities to become who we're meant to be.

This moment feels electric, alive with potential. It's not just another chapter; it's a bold, passionate leap into the unknown. A chance to rewrite the rules, to create, to love, and to live more deeply than ever before.

I carry forward the lessons of the past—the laughter, the tears, the love—and I hold them close as I step into this new beginning. Life has shown me that it's not the destination that defines us; it's the fire in our hearts, the courage to keep going, and the passion to embrace each new day as if it were our first.

This is my next chapter, and it's bursting with life. The story isn't over—it's only just beginning. And as long as there's breath in me, I'll keep writing it with everything I've got. The journey continues, and I'm ready to make it the most extraordinary adventure yet

Chapter 97: The Next Adventure Awaits

So, what's my next adventure, you may ask? Well, we'll just have to wait and see. If there's one thing I've learned about life, it's that it's utterly unpredictable—and that's exactly what makes it so exhilarating. You never know what's around the corner, what surprise is waiting to shake things up, or what opportunity might appear when you least expect it.

What could possibly go wrong, you wonder? Well, stick around—because if my journey has taught me anything, it's that life has a way of keeping you on your toes. The twists, the turns, the unexpected bumps—they're not obstacles; they're part of the thrill. They're what make the story worth telling.

Whatever comes next, I'm ready for it. Whether it's a new challenge, a dream I didn't know I had, or a path I never thought I'd walk, I'll face it head-on. Life is an adventure, after all—and the best part is, the adventure never truly ends.

Chapter 98: A Life of Twists, Turns, and Transformations; The Journey of Creation

Life, they say, is unpredictable—but if you've walked even a mile in my shoes, you'd know that doesn't begin to cover it. My journey has been anything but ordinary. I've taken paths I never saw coming, from engineering—a world of precision and structure—to the boundless depths of hypnoanalysis, where the mind becomes the playground for transformation.

From there, I found myself teaching hypnosis, unlocking the doors of possibility for others. And then, somehow, I became an author. Seven books. Yes, seven! Can you believe it? Sometimes I can't.

But here's the thing: I don't think of myself as a writer. Far from it. I've always felt like the words don't come from me but through me, as though some greater force whispers them into my soul. I'm just the vessel, the slightly mad, wildly passionate lunatic who dares to listen and let the words flow.

Because that's what writing feels like; an act of listening, of surrendering to something far greater than yourself.

It's led me to create something I'm deeply proud of: **Inherited Therapy** and **The Loveday Method**—concepts that are reshaping how we think about healing. They've been trademarked worldwide, but their reach goes far beyond a name or a technique.

They dive into the very fabric of human experience, tackling **transgenerational trauma**—the invisible wounds that pass down through families, shaping lives before we're even aware of them.

It's not just psychology; it's a revelation. The idea that we can untangle the past to free the future? That we can stop carrying pain that isn't ours to bear? That's powerful.

And yet, even as I write this, I know my story is still being written. Life has a way of surprising you when you least expect it, doesn't it?

Every twist and turn, every so-called detour, has brought me here—to a place where I can make a real difference. A place where I can help people find their way out of darkness they didn't know was theirs.

What's next? I couldn't tell you—and that's the beauty of it. Life doesn't give us a map, only a compass and the courage to keep going.

But if my past is anything to go by, I know one thing for certain; the road ahead will be wild, meaningful, and utterly extraordinary. And I'm ready for every step of it. Are you?

Chapter 99: From the Heart; A Life Lived, A Story Told

"This book I've written isn't just a collection of words or stories—it's a piece of my soul, poured straight from the heart. It's not crafted from the mind, polished and calculated; it's raw, authentic, and deeply personal. Every chapter is infused with the emotions, experiences, and lessons that have shaped my journey. It's not about perfection or technique—it's about truth, vulnerability, and the profound connection we share through the stories of life. This isn't just a book; it's a reflection of who I am and everything I've lived."

"71 Years Young: The Adventure Continues"

"There you have it—I'm 71 years young, still embracing life boldly, unapologetically, and entirely on my own terms. It's funny, really, because deep down, I still feel like that wide-eyed, adventurous 10-year-old, brimming with wonder, mischief, and an insatiable curiosity for what's next. Life has thrown its fair share of challenges my way, but every single one has only stoked the fire within me. As far as I'm concerned, the journey isn't slowing down—it's just getting started, and the best, most exciting chapters are yet to be written."

So now you're probably thinking, "Surely this is it, right? There can't possibly be more books to write?" Oh, sweet summer child, you bet your life there are! This is just the opening act. If you thought this was chaotic, brace yourself—because my life seems to be on a permanent loop of "Hold my beer and watch this."

Simon, my daughters, my bizarre choices, and a constant stream of unexpected disasters? Honestly, it's like the universe has me starring in a never-ending sitcom. So yes, more books are coming, because let's face it, my life keeps handing me material. Grab a snack and settle in—this is just the trailer for the madness yet to come!

Chapter 100: A New Beginning: The Magic of a Life Well Lived

I once believed this was the end of my story, the final chapter in a life that had run its course. Yet as I sit here, pen in hand, heart wide open, I now see the truth: this is not an ending, but a glorious beginning. Looking back, my life reveals itself as a tapestry of wonder and resilience—woven with threads of moments both extraordinary and humbling.

It has been nothing short of magical. The challenges, the triumphs, and the quiet in-between moments all come together to tell a story I never fully appreciated until now. Above all, I am overwhelmed with gratitude for the incredible people who have graced my journey. They've enriched my life in ways I could never have imagined, their presence a gift I cherish deeply.

I've been blessed to witness their stories unfold and to have been part of their lives, as they have been part of mine. Each connection, each shared moment, has left an indelible mark on my soul. This realization fills me with awe and a renewed sense of purpose for whatever lies ahead. The future is no longer a blank page but a canvas waiting for the next brushstroke.

This is not the end—it is the dawn of something greater, a continuation of the magic I now see so clearly.

I'm leaving Simon's email here.[1] Why? Because if I'm being dragged through the fiery pits of fitness hell, I'm not going alone. Misery loves company, and trust me,

Simon will make you very miserable.

---

[1] simonwilkes26@yahoo.co.uk

www.ingramcontent.com/pod-product-compliance
Lightning Source LLC
Chambersburg PA
CBHW072043110526
44590CB00018B/3015